THE MURDER OF THORA CHAMBERLAIN

A Shocking True Crime Story

Rod Kackley

Lyons Circle Publishing Inc.

Copyright © 2021 Lyons Circle Publishing Inc.

All rights reserved

No part of this book may be reproduced, or stored in a retrieval system, or transmitted in any form or by any means, electronic, mechanical, photocopying, recording, or otherwise, without express written permission of the publisher.

Cover design by: SelfPubBookCovers.com/ Daniela

"I say a murder is abstract. You pull the trigger and after that, you do not understand anything that happens."

JEAN PAUL SARTRE

CONTENTS

Title Page
Copyright
Epigraph
Chapter 1   1
Chapter 2   4
Chapter 3   7
Chapter 4   10
Chapter 5   14
Chapter 6   16
Chapter 7   18
Chapter 8   20
Chapter 9   23
Chapter 10   25
Chapter 11   29
Chapter 12   33
Chapter 13   37
Chapter 14   41
Chapter 15   44
Chapter 16   46
Chapter 17   50
Chapter 18   54

Chapter 19	57
Chapter 20	61
Chapter 21	65
Chapter 22	68
Chapter 23	70
Chapter 24	73
Chapter 25	75
Chapter 26	77
Chapter 27	79
Chapter 28	81
Chapter 29	83
Chapter 30	85
Chapter 31	88
Chapter 32	91
Chapter 33	95
Chapter 34	97
Chapter 35	99
Chapter 36	101
Chapter 37	104
Chapter 38	107
Chapter 39	109
Chapter 40	111
Chapter 41	113
Chapter 42	116
Chapter 43	119
Chapter 44	121
Chapter 45	126
Chapter 46	129

Chapter 47	132
Chapter 48	136
Chapter 49	140
Chapter 50	142
Chapter 51	147
Chapter 52	150
Chapter 53	153
Chapter 54	156
Chapter 55	159
Chapter 56	162
Chapter 57	165
Chapter 58	169
Chapter 59	172
Chapter 60	175
Chapter 61	178
Chapter 62	181
Chapter 63	184
Chapter 64	188
Chapter 65	192
Chapter 66	196
Chapter 67	200
Chapter 68	203
Chapter 69	204
Chapter 70	207
Chapter 71	210
Chapter 72	214
Chapter 73	218
Bibliography	220

| About The Author | 227 |
| Books By This Author | 229 |

CHAPTER 1

September 21, 1945

World War II is finally over and done with. America celebrated V-J day a month ago and Victory in Europe a few months earlier, in May.

The war can't be forgotten, though, not yet.

Thanks to Operation Magic Carpet, the post-World War II operation to bring U.S. military personnel home, millions of servicemen from the Pacific Theater are streaming back home through California.

So military uniforms, including those of the U.S. Navy, are hardly unfamiliar.

Even before soldiers, marines, sailors, and airmen started arriving, the Navy has had a strong presence in Campbell, California, for the past four years. The small town exploding with this new population is relatively close to the Pacific Ocean, only five miles from San Jose and forty-two miles from San Francisco.

One of those returning through California is Petty Officer John Cooper. After being stationed in London and Ireland as a chief commissary steward in the U.S. Naval Reserve, Cooper is back home on American soil.

"Damn it, someone's nicked my footlocker," Cooper yells only a few minutes after getting off duty and returning for some R&R in his quarters.

"What," asks a fellow sailor, "are you talking about?"

Cooper, his fair skin under his blonde hair going scarlet

rustration, stops himself. Fists clenched, he remembers to speak American and not British.

"Nicked, damn it, stolen."

"Your footlocker?"

"Yes, for Christ's sake. What did I just say?"

"Don't blaspheme," orders Petty Officer Mark Carrier, a devout Christian who's also just returned from overseas.

"Sorry," says Cooper. "But for Pete's sake, then, some SOB has swiped my footlocker."

"You didn't just misplace it," says Carrier.

"Oh, Jimmy Christmas," Cooper says. "How the fucking hell would I misplace a four-foot-long footlocker?"

"Hey, don't ask me," says a third player in the melodrama, "it's above my pay grade."

Carrier gets off his bunk and walks toward Cooper, intending to console his buddy. Lots of their fellow anchor flankers who spent so much time overseas came home like walking land mines. Say the wrong thing, and they'll go off. Cooper hadn't seen combat, but Carrier could be sure the wages of war had rubbed off on him.

"Any money in it?"

Cooper, getting on grip on himself, finally shakes his head to indicate there wasn't a dime inside the locker.

"Then don't lose your cool over it."

"Yeah, but I had important stuff in it."

"Like?"

"Like, my white Londonderry, Ireland, Navy t-shirt. My medals are pinned on it, then there is my Navy slate-gray trousers, now missing."

Carrier rubs his chin. Nobody wants to lose their navy garb because it's too damn hard to replace. And those medals; the last thing you want is some damn civilian wearing what you earned.

After thinking a few ticks, Cooper says, "and there was my garrison hat. That was in the footlocker too."

Carrier puts both hands on Cooper's shoulders. "Tough luck, buddy. But, hey, let's go into town, find us a couple of local dames, and have some fun."

Now that he's had his say, Cooper's complexion is fading from red hot to freckled pale. And he thinks that some time spent with a khaki wacky, a broad who loves a man, any man in uniform, might not be so bad.

CHAPTER 2

November 2, 1945

The waitress, Sally, is getting more than a little weary of watching a guy wearing a white T-shirt with blue insignia bearing the words "Londonderry, Ireland," playing the Big Broadcast pinball machine.

She's come to understand that servicemen returning to the U.S. have nothing but time on their hands until they either ship out again or hop a bus back home.

Some of these guys are more than a bit of doll dizzy and can't keep their hands to themselves. But this fellow, even though he has thick, wavy black hair and a friendly grin, is not much more than a cold fish.

He's had his lunch — hamburger, fries, and chocolate shake — but doesn't have the slightest interest in leaving. Sally saw him pull up in an old blue sedan, still parked in front of the Cozy Cafe. So it's not like he's waiting for a lift.

But she thinks he must be waiting for something, just standing at the counter dropping coins into that damn pinball game.

Such a simple game. You pull the plunger back, shoot a metal ball up into the game, and it either bounces around and lands in a hole labeled for a city like Detroit, and you score some points, or it falls down.

Five balls for a nickel. It's a way to kill time waiting for lunch, but beyond that, nobody but some dumb kids play Big Broadcast like this guy's playing it.

Louis, the boss, keeps moving closer to the guy, giving him the wicked eye, rubbing the lunch counter harder and faster than he has to, trying to give this fathead the message that it's time to take a powder and hit the road.

"What's buzzin' cousin?" Louis tries to strike up a conversation with the guy but gets nothing in return except a dead, fish-eye look along with that silly smile pasted on his face.

Well, Louis figures, at least he's not shaking the game or tilting it from side to side. Big Broadcast has been a license to print nickels at the Cozy, and with all the factories still in wartime production, a new pinball game would not be easy to get.

At least this knucklehead isn't destroying it. So, his nickels are as good as anyone's and better than some.

Yet, there is something about him that bothers Louis.

Sally tries too.

Usually, she doesn't have any trouble striking up a chat with the lonely, war-exhausted GIs who camp out in Campbell until they're homeward bound or redeployed.

With her flaming red hair, she gets all the lines like "Hey sugar. Are you rationed?" And Sally's overheard the whispered debate about whether her carpet matches the drapes. Like any of these clowns are ever going to find out.

Nobody knows that secret except her husband, Tommy.

December 5, 1941, Tommy and Sally got married.

Two days later, they're still in Campbell, waiting to leave for their honeymoon on Monday. Sunday, they decide to go see a picture at the Campbell Theater.

It's a good one, two of Sally's favorite stars, Clark Gable and Lana Turner, in a movie called "Honky Tonk."

Tommy and Sally cuddle as close as two honeymooners can without getting a room —giggling, swapping popcorn, and Tommy's hands are all over Sally — when the movie stops.

Right in the middle, the lights come on, and the theater's manager walks out on stage.

Mr. Swanson tells everyone the Japs bombed Pearl Harbor.

Sally doesn't know where that is, but she knows enough about the fighting in Europe and the Pacific to figure out what's going on.

Tommy gets a look on her face Sally hasn't seen since Billy Cousino tried to dance with her at a Campbell Union High sock hop a couple of years ago. Tommy grabs Sally's hand. They rise from their seats and wait impatiently while the crowd files out of the theater.

Once outside, Tommy tells Sally to "wait here" and walks across the street into a U.S. Army Recruiting Station.

A month later, he is gone, overseas in the U.S. Army Air Corps. Tommy wasn't going to be a pilot; Sally felt better about that; he'd be a mechanic on the ground. She promised to wait for him.

A year later, a telegram came notifying Sally that she'd have to wait forever.

Sure, there's a tear in Sally's eye as she's thinking about this, looking at this navy guy who's been at her counter since noon.

It's just after two now, and the high school kids are starting to stream in, so there's no time to be a sad sack.

Sally gets back to work, and while she's taking an order looks out the front window and sees the blue sedan pulling away.

A quick glance at the counter, and Sally sees the navy veteran is gone. On to bigger and better things, she figures.

CHAPTER 3

2:35 P.M.

Like every school day, two sisters, Carole Anne and Yvonne Rappe, aged seven and eight years respectively, are walking home together from the Campbell Grammar School, across the street from the high school.

The "war," as their parents called it, had brought hundreds of thousands of young families to California, and many of them set up housekeeping in Campbell.

So, when Carole Anne and Yvonne walk home from school together, they are usually part of a long parade of other grammar school kids.

As a matter of fact, there were so many kids in Campbell, on Halloween night, last month, you couldn't swing a trick-or-treat bag without bumping into one of the girls' classmates.

So, Yvonne and Carole Anne have plenty of company, most days on their way home from school.

But, not today.

They offered to help their favorite teacher, Mr. Bentley, clean the blackboard after class this afternoon. He accepted, and the girls had spent a half-hour wiping off the board, banging erasers together outside the school, and generally having a good time.

Neither Carole Anne nor Yvonne noticed the noise of the kids leaving school, some hopping on board the yellow school buses, others walking home.

As a matter of fact, most days, the cacophony of children went unnoticed by those orchestrating the din of noise.

However, now, walking home, the silence is deafening. Carole Anne, the younger of the pair, has two of her fingers in her mouth.

It is babyish, but the neighborhood has never seemed so monstrous as it does this minute.

Yvonne might have been only eight months her senior, but she can tell Carole Anne is scared. So she does what any big sister would do; she reaches out and takes the younger girl's hand.

They smile and skip the rest of the way home. Until that is, they hear two beeps from a car's horn.

Both girls stop. There is no reason to be afraid. Neither girl is aware that anyone in the world would want to hurt them. The thought never crosses their minds.

So, curiosity being what it is, Yvonne and Carole Anne walk toward the blue sedan. Inside the car is a smiling man, a grown-up, wearing a white T-shirt and a hat with a visor.

Nothing about this man is different from the soldiers, marines, and sailors the girls see every day.

"Hi girls, how are you?"

Yvonne and Carole Anne giggle.

"Hey, can you help me?"

Now he has their attention. Children like these two girls are always willing to help a grown-up.

The man smiles and leans out the window of his car.

"I need someone to help me babysit my little girl. She's about your age. Do you want to play with us?"

Yvonne thinks this is a great idea. Playing with a new friend would be much better than going home; it would be an excellent new adventure, if nothing else.

But Carole Anne, even though she's the younger of the pair, knows something is wrong. It isn't that she's shy; it's just that she does not want to get into this man's car.

She grabs Yvonne's hand, pulls as hard as her seven-year-old self can, and starts running.

Yvonne looks back over her shoulder to wave goodbye and sees the man doing a U-turn in the street and driving back toward the school where the big kids go, Campbell Union High.

CHAPTER 4

3:00 P.M.

Thora Chamberlain and her friends are walking to a football game between Campbell Union High School, which the girls attend, and Washington High School of Centerville.

Only twenty days short of her fifteenth birthday, Thora, with brown hair and blue eyes, stands five feet two inches tall and weighs 120 pounds.

She's wearing a gabardine coat, a blue sweater, a white blouse, a red skirt, and just like her friends, two pairs of overlapping bobby socks — one red, the other colored blue— on each foot, and tan loafers.

And, again, like the other girls, Thora's carrying textbooks, a zippered binder, and a cowbell to ring in support of the Campbell Union team.

Thora fits right in with her friends, but she is undoubtedly the leader of this pack.

The girls are already having fun. Laughing, talking over each other, smiling, and even skipping to the football game.

Why not? The school week is over.

But more than that, like the rest of America, Thora and her friends are finally over the Second World War.

All they can talk about is getting to the game, ringing their cowbells, and talking to the boys.

Two of Thora's friends -- Elaine Scimeca and Catherine Ban -- both fifteen years old with blonde hair and green eyes, are the first to see the car. It's a blue Plymouth slowly coming up alongside the girls on Winchester Boulevard.

Elaine and Catherine think it looks like one of those cars the gangsters drove in the movies.

It's old, but that is nothing out of the norm across America. Since the auto plants converted to military manufacturing in 1942, nobody's been able to buy anything new from General Motors, Ford, or Chrysler for close to three years.

However, there is one thing unusual about this car. It is creeping up alongside Thora and her friends and stops when the girls halt.

Looking at one of her older friends, Rita Bieler, standing right beside her, Thora hopes for guidance from the seventeen-year-old.

But receiving none, Thora giggles and shrugs her shoulders. Never shy but still cautious, Thora looks back for reassurance. Nobody signals for her to stop, so she presses on.

Just as Thora moves a couple steps closer to the Plymouth, the guy inside reaches over and rolls down the passenger side window.

"Hi, ladies."

While her friends nervously laugh, Thora takes two steps back and then one step forward.

"Hi yourself," she says.

Like the car, this guy isn't the worst she's ever seen. About thirty years old. Which, of course, is "darn old," Thora thinks that's what she'll say later when she and her friends are huddled under the bleachers at the game smoking cigarettes.

But still, he is a guy, and Thora's been finding herself more attracted to boys and men, especially men, than ever.

And, he's got the thick, wavy black hair that Thora just loves, along with a quick, easy, kind of goofy smile.

He's wearing a garrison hat with a water-repellent cover and a U.S. Navy-style white t-shirt with a Purple Heart and blue insignia bearing the words "Londonderry, Ireland."

Pinned on the shirt are several service medals.

It's hardly unusual to see ex-sailors, soldiers, marines, and airmen wandering the streets of Campbell. Millions of World War II vets are being repatriated through a network of depots and de-embarkation centers. That includes more than 800,000 Californians returning home from the war.

And many can't find work. The state's unemployment rate is destined to hit 8.8% next year, compared to the nation's 3.9% jobless rate.

So neither Thora, Elaine, Catherine, or Rita are shocked to see a navy veteran driving around town.

All in all, he seems more than worth talking with, at least in the eyes of a soon-to-be fifteen-year-old girl, like Thora.

She moves even closer and bends over a bit to look through the passenger window. He puts the car in neutral, not bothering to turn off the motor, but sets the parking brake.

The man clears his throat. Thora thinks he looks a little nervous too. The other girls move up behind her, close enough to hear the conversation.

"I was wondering if you could help me out," the man says with a grin, winning a return smile from Thora before his gaze shifts from her blue eyes to the green eyes of her friends standing behind.

Then his attention shifts back to Thora, making her feel like there's no one else in the world but the two of them.

She lifts an eyebrow and waits for him to continue.

"Well, here's the thing. I need someone to babysit my sister's kid. A baby, no trouble at all. He'll probably sleep for the rest of the afternoon."

Thora lifts her eyebrows and says, "sorry, we're all going to the football game."

"I know, I know. So, I would really appreciate this, that's why," the man reaches into the front pocket of slate-grey U.S. Navy trousers and pulls out a five-dollar bill. "I'm ready to pay you."

Now, this gets the girls' attention, especially Thora's. Five dollars buys a lot of fun in Campbell.

But there's the football game.

"I'd only need you for about thirty minutes. My sister and I just need to run a couple of errands. No more than half an hour, I promise. And, then, I will drive you to the football game. You'll be there by halftime."

He folds the bill and rubs the fiver between his thumb and forefinger, lifting an eyebrow again, looking damn cute to Thora.

"What do you say? Easy money, right?"

He holds the money close to the rolled-down window and smiles.

Taking a deep breath, Thora looks back at her friends. She's made a lot of money babysitting for mothers whose husbands are overseas. So, Thora's up for the job. But first, she looks back again at her friends.

No takers. What the heck, she figures, five bucks is five bucks.

"Save me a seat, will ya. See you in thirty," Thora says over her shoulder.

She snatches the fin out of the man's hand. They both laugh as he pushes the passenger side door open, and Thora jumps in.

He drops the Plymouth into first, quickly pulling away, with Thora laughing and waving to her friends.

"Don't forget to save me a seat," Thora yells out the window, "see you soon."

CHAPTER 5

3:30 P.M.

Ella Ribble Beaudoux, the wife of a San Jose physician, an eye specialist, goes out to get her mail from the roadside mailbox outside her home in Saratoga, less than six miles southwest of Campbell.

While her husband is locally famous in his own right, Ella's made a name for herself, too, as a musical composer.

A locally famous soprano in Oakland, Marie Wallman, included one of Ella's songs, 'Bonnie Nuit,' in a song recital at Hotel Oakland ten years ago.

Then in 1936, the pianist, Helen Wegman Parmelle, devoted her fifteen-minute program on KLX radio to Ella's compositions of light classics.

Several of those compositions were accepted by a publishing house in the East.

Some of Ella's compositions were also sung by local musicians in 1937 during a garden club exhibition in Berkeley.

However, during the war, her priorities, like those of most Californian's changed dramatically.

And today, Ella's mission is much more mundane than it might have been a decade ago.

It's time to start dinner — her husband should be home in two hours, and he expects the evening meal to be nearly ready for the table when he arrives.

Yet, it is also time to get the mail from her small family's roadside mailbox.

Ella steps off the lawn. She puts a foot in the street and gets ready to turn to the mailbox when a blue car speeds by, coming down the highway from Los Gatos, and nearly runs her down. Ella only manages to avoid falling flat on the ground by hanging on to the mailbox.

As she slips and goes down before catching herself, Ella looks directly into the car. Through the passenger side window, Ella's mind's eye takes a virtual snapshot of what's inside the coupe.

It's a picture Ella will never forget.

She sees a teenage girl, young, with bouncy curls in her brown hair, wearing a red skirt and a blue sweater. The child's face is pressed against the car's window as she claws furiously at the glass, trying desperately to get out.

Beyond the girl, Ella sees a man, hatless, with bushy hair driving with both hands on the steering wheel.

Ella lets go of the mailbox handle and sits down on the lawn. Her head falls forward as she tries to catch her breath.

Then, she looks up, realizing she'll never forget that girl's face because Ella has never seen such fear.

CHAPTER 6

5:00 p.m.

An hour into the game against Washington High, it's halftime. Parents, teachers, and students swarm the concession stands across from the bleachers.

Quick game, so far. Not many penalties considering twenty-two high school kids are on the field. Not much of a score either. But neither Elaine, Catherine, Rita, nor any of Thora's other close friends cares much about the score or the action on the field.

Especially not now.

The girls mill about the concourse, chatting up as many of their friends as possible. They're even talking to some of the boys when courage allows.

Rita can see the scoreboard clock over Elaine's shoulder. It's counting down the minutes and seconds left in halftime, showing fans when they need to get back to their seats.

"Hey, we only have a couple of minutes left before the game starts again," Rita says and takes a sip of her Coca-Cola.

Catherine laughs and breaks off a conversation with Luke Bailey, a guy she's been interested in since teaming up with him at a freshman chemistry lab table.

She lifts a sarcastic eyebrow Rita's way. "Like I care?"

Elaine, another of the group, who, like Rita, is still building the courage to talk to boys the way Catherine does.

She shrugs her shoulders.

Elaine couldn't care less about football, but Rita wouldn't mind sitting down again. So she takes Elaine by the arm, and together they leave Catherine with Luke and start walking back to the grandstand.

One more of the gang, Karen, runs up to Elaine and Rita, trying not to spill her popcorn as she runs, eats, and dodges other students.

"Hey," Karen says after helping herself to a sip of Rita's soda. "Where's Thora?"

CHAPTER 7

7:30 p.m.

The sounds of the marching bands from Campbell Union faded away at least an hour ago, Thora's mother thinks to herself, and still, there's no sign of her daughter.

Frank and Lois Chamberlain weren't expecting Thora to be home for their usual 5:30 p.m. dinner. But now, the food Lois set aside for Thora has been wrapped in foil for two hours, and there is still no sign of the girl.

Frank, reading his newspaper in the living room, mutters, "Have you tried calling her friends?"

Her forehead wrinkled with a worried frown, Lois puts her finger in the circular dial of the rectangular black phone hung on the kitchen wall by the milk chute and begins dialing.

One of Thora's friends picks up on the third ring.

"No, Mrs. Chamberlain," says Rita, "Thora never came to the football game. At least we didn't see her."

"She didn't go to the game?"

"No, ma'am."

"Why not?"

Rita took a moment to take a bite of a cookie as Lois's stomach churned. What had happened to Thora?

"Well?" Lois asks.

Rita swallows and savors the taste of the Toll House Chocolate Chip cookie she'd made herself.

Finally, she says, "We were all on our way to the game, walking down Winchester when a car pulled up."

"And?"

"Thora got in, and they drove off."

"Oh my God," Lois gasps. She quickly says goodbye out of politeness more than anything else and hangs up.

Lois begins dialing again.

One of Thora's friends after another, all of whom had arrived at their homes by 7 p.m., tell Lois the story of how Thora had gotten into a blue car and driven off, never to return.

"Frank!" Lois slams the phone's receiver back into its holder hard enough to be heard by her husband and runs into the living room.

At first, annoyed by the interruption of his reading of the sports pages, Frank's attitude changes as he soaks in the fear and panic on Lois's face.

He crumbles the newspaper more than folds it, tossing it aside.

Frank was too old to serve in the war, but he sees himself as a man of action. The town agrees. Frank is a well-respected businessman in Campbell,

With that attitude, Frank quickly, yet firmly, hugs Lois on his way to the kitchen before sticking his finger in the dial on the black phone.

As soon as the connection is made, and thank God nobody's on the party line, Frank demands to speak with the chief of police.

Less than half an hour later, Frank, Lois, and as many neighbors as they can round up, with more joining them as the night wears on, walk through the streets of Campbell calling out, in vain, Thora's name.

CHAPTER 8

November 3, 1945

This morning, Thomas Henry McMonigle returns to work as a laborer at Blair's construction yard in Burlingame, thirty-five miles north of Campbell.

Thomas's buddies are usually glad to see him, of course. Thomas is always good for a joke, a laugh, and a slap on the back. And he's not a bad worker either, as long as the foreman makes sure Thomas is given explicit instructions and is watched like a hawk.

However, his reception today is a bit on the chilly side. While Thomas is a great guy to be around, he's never been the most responsible man on the crew.

He's ducked out early quite often, maybe more often than the rest of the crew. But Thomas has always punched in close to on-time and has never left more than half-an-hour early.

However, this time, he's been off work, absent without leave, if you will, for the past five days, Monday through Friday of last week.

You wouldn't know, however, he'd done anything wrong by watching Thomas enter the construction yard.

Ever the cocky master manipulator, with the muscles and coordination of the boxer he was as a teenager, Thomas swaggers up to the time clock at 7:55 a.m., a full five minutes early to begin his shift. He listens to the clock clunking along as his buddies punch in for work. When Thomas gets up to the clock to take his turn, he runs his right index and forefingers down the time cards.

No surprise his card is missing. It's happened before when Thomas has taken one of his little vacations.

Thomas smiles at his co-workers, promises to be "right back," and jogs across the hard dirt of the yard to the boss's trailer.

Respectfully, he knocks on the door and waits for the boss to shout, "Come!"

Thomas takes off his hat and sticks his head in the door, throwing one of his trademark smiles inside.

The boss groans and tosses a pencil down on the papers covering his gray, steel desk.

"Do I know you?"

Thomas, holding his hat in his hand, takes one tentative step inside, then another.

"Yeah, of course, you do, boss. It's me, Thomas McMonigle."

The boss leans back in his wooden swivel chair. "Oh yeah, I remember you. You're the rat bastard who took a powder and left me hanging five days in a row last week. Can't believe you got the moxie to show up today, or are you just plain stupid?"

"My mom, she was sick, couldn't help it."

"Oh, for Christ's sake." The boss leaps from his chair with an agility no one his size should possess. An easy six-foot-three inches tall and packed with more than two hundred pounds of solid muscle, he proves the cliche that the bosses of construction crews always fight their way to the top.

Thomas takes a step back out of respect without showing a scintilla of fear. It's not like he's never battled a man bigger than himself.

Thomas shrugs and tosses a shy smile the boss's way.

"I know I should have called or left word with one of the other guys, boss. And I do apologize, but I was so torn up about my mom, well, you know."

The boss moves two steps closer to Thomas. He's madder than a wet hen, but he's facing a deadline and needs every hand he can get for the next two weeks.

"So she's better?"

"Who? What?"

"Your mother, dumb shit!"

"Oh yeah, excellent now, you know."

The boss glowers at Thomas, then reaches under one of the piles of spreadsheets on his desk. He comes out of the mess with a time card.

Thomas smiles when he sees his name scrawled in pencil at the top of the card. Moving quickly, so the boss doesn't have a chance to change his mind and take a swing at him with one of those fists made of concrete, Thomas snatches the card and moves toward the door.

"Thanks, boss, won't let you down."

The boss can't help but laugh. Hard to find good help at forty-cents-an-hour, and with all the good men still overseas, he is stuck with the fat heads, flat-foots, and the Thomas Henry McMonigles of the world.

Thomas resumes his old swagger as he waltzes to the time clock and hears the satisfying clunk of the clock registering that he's starting his day.

Putting his hat on his head at a jaunty angle, he walks up to his buddies.

Back slaps and hard shoulder punches are exchanged before the foreman yells more than a few appropriate curses and threats, and the gang of six gets to work.

Another thirty minutes into what will be a back-breaking ten-hour day, one of the crew yells over to Thomas, "so where the hell were you anyway?"

Thomas leans on his shovel, tips his hat back with his left thumb, and smiles.

"Out with a fifteen-year-old girl, that's where. And oh yeah, a real cookie, she was!"

CHAPTER 9

November 6, 1945

The construction yard boss can't believe it. For the past couple of days, that cockeyed, knucklehead McMonigle has been after him to do extra work.

"Can you believe it?" the boss shakes his head as Thomas's foreman stands beside him, examining the results of Thomas's efforts.

"We gotta build a small ramp or causeway over this ditch," Thomas pleaded the second day after he returned from his unpaid, five-day vacation.

"Why?"

Thomas looks his boss in the eye. "Because, boss, if we can walk over the ditch instead of around it, we'll save all kinds of time and effort."

Much as he hated to admit it, that was a good idea, almost worthy of management. But why take a chance, the boss thought the next day.

"If you do your usual half-ass job or decide to take a powder two hours into it, what am I left with?

The boss squinted into the sun as he looked at Thomas and rolled the dice in his mind.

"You do that, and I'll have to move someone else off the crew to finish it."

"Won't happen, I guarantee it."

"You are going to do it all by your lonesome? You are going to fill this ditch with dirt and concrete blocks?"

Before Thomas could say a word, the boss shook his head and walked away.

But the next day, after another half-hour of pleading, whining, and promises, the boss did something he hardly ever does. He gave in and granted Thomas permission to leave the crew for a day to start and finish this project.

"Eight hours, that's all you get, understand?"

"Absolutely boss. No problem, natch, it will be done."

So now, here it is, 5 p.m., and Thomas has proven himself to be on the beam. He rests on a shovel and fixes his foreman and the yard boss with a dirty, sweaty smile.

And as the Planet Earth stops spinning on its axis for a moment, the yard boss smiles at Thomas.

"Good job. See you tomorrow."

CHAPTER 10

6:25 P.M.

Thomas arrives at the home in San Mateo he shares with his wife, Ena, exhausted. Thinking about it, as he parks his blue two-door in the driveway, Thomas realizes today is the first in a long time when he actually put in a full day's work.

Turning the key in the front door lock, Thomas doesn't know quite what to expect because there is a newborn baby in the house.

A beautiful girl, born last month, on October 30, if you want to be exact about it, Thomas might tell anyone who will listen.

He's as proud as any new papa might be, but let's face it. Nothing changes a life like a new life.

The big question on Thomas's mind as he turns the key: Will the kid be sleeping or squawking?

He slowly turns the key and opens the door. He holds his breath and listens.

Thomas sighs. All's quiet on the western front. Coast clear. At least for now.

Ena's in the living room, singing along with the radio, their Crosley solid-wood floor model. Has to be at least seven years old. Thomas came home with it one day, riding in the bed of his buddy's Ford pickup truck. Ena knew better than to ask how he'd come by the radio. She was just happy to be able to hear music at night.

This evening, Ena might be singing along with Les Brown and Doris Day's version of Sentimental Journey — it has been a hit since March — but she is as dog-tired as her husband.

He might have spent the day digging a ditch, but Ena spent hers behind the counter at Woolworth's. That's no easy task either.

So it is with less than honeymoon joy that she greets Thomas this early evening.

"Hello to you, too," Thomas says in answer to her grunt as he walks in the door.

Pall Mall hanging out of her mouth with a good half-inch of ash, Ena winks and leads Thomas into the kitchen. There they sit at a small Formica table, just big enough for the two of them, and dine on the hamburgers she'd started cooking a few minutes ago.

Thomas picks at his food. He lifts the burger to his mouth, barely takes a bit, and puts it back down. Ena's made fries too. He uses the small potatoes to draw a picture in the ketchup on his plate.

Ena's talking, unprompted, about her day at Woolworth's and how much her feet hurt. Hearing no response, she looks up from her food at Thomas. His eyes remind her of the drug addicts she sees every day as she walks from the bus stop to her store.

She taps her fork on the edge of her plate.

Nothing. No response.

"Hello!"

"Huh?"

Ena sits back and folds her arms across her chest. She moves her head so that she can look Thomas in the eye.

"You like?"

"Huh?"

"Hamburgers. Did you like them?"

"Oh, sure. Great. Killer diller." Thomas gets up from the table, flashes her the smile Ena fell in love with, and leans down to give her a kiss on the cheek.

"You're an ace," he says before delivering a not-so-playful slap on her cheek.

Ena puts her hand to her cheek, blinks back a tear, and smiles.

"Thanks a bunch."

She takes a deep breath and watches Thomas walk back into the living room. He's putting on his jacket. What the heck?

Ena forgets the dirty dishes and plants her hands firmly on her hips. With a fresh Pall Mall between her lips, she says, "You're taking a powder already?"

"Love to stick around, you know that." Thomas smiles from the living room, his hand on the front doorknob.

"Oh no! You're not going out again. Not tonight!"

"Listen, babe, I gotta go. Got business."

"Oh yeah, what business?" Ena lights a new Pall Mall off the one that had been in her mouth before stubbing the first out in a glass ashtray she'd bought on sale from the Grants' Five and Dime.

"Just business." Thomas tightens his grip on the doorknob, but at the same time, flashes her the smile he knows Ena loves. Or at least she did the night they met at the dance hall.

"Just business. Of course, you can't talk about it."

Thomas releases the doorknob and throws his hands into the air.

"Do you really want to know?"

The truth of it is, no, Ena doesn't want to know.

So, she responds to his question without a direct answer and says in a much calmer voice, "can you at least tell me where you're going?"

"Sure, doll." Thomas smiles again and reaches for the doorknob.

"L.A."

"L.A.? As in Los Angeles, L.A.?"

"It's like you're reading the map in my head."

"And you're going to be back home; when?"

"Soon as possible, you know that."

"Yeah, I know that only too well."

"See ya!"

Thomas tosses his car keys to Ena and moves out the door with the grace of the boxer he was fifteen years ago. And, quick as that, he's gone.

While Ena is tapping another cigarette to get the tobacco packed nicely, Thomas is close to running down the street. He sees the bus to Los Angeles and starts a full sprint.

He's got to get to L.A. It's mandatory. And after that, your guess is as good as mine; Thomas might tell Ena if she were here.

But right now, I just gotta get out of California, Thomas thinks.

Then, with the ferocity and certainty of a jail cell door swinging shut, his mind is made up. A bus will get him to Los Angeles.

Once there, Thomas will just stick out his thumb and see how far he can go. It is tougher to get a ride these days than it was when Thomas was a kid. People are too afraid of getting robbed or murdered.

But there is something about Thomas that makes people trust him or take a chance on him. And, now that he's left the Plymouth with Ena, what choice does he have?

Maybe I'll wind up in East Alton, Illinois, Thomas thinks, and drop in on the dear, old family.

CHAPTER 11

November 8, 1945

It's been six excruciatingly long days and nights for Frank and Lois Chamberlain, who, along with their two other daughters, wait by their phone for the call that tells them Thora's been found alive and well.

Or the alternative.

But hope springs eternal.

Neighbors still walk the streets of the Chamberlain family's neighborhood, today searching in vain for Thora. But the vanguard of the effort to find the missing girl has fallen on the shoulders of local police.

Those officers may not be working alone for long, however. Assistance could soon be coming from Washington, whether the local authorities want it or not.

The FBI will be put on the case since the disappearance of Thora Chamberlain is probably a kidnapping case that might have already crossed state lines.

But maybe the feds will be able to stay home.

Speculation grows today that Thora is doing okay, or at the very least, will be found in the Long Beach area.

San Jose Evening News editors are looking at a telegram they've received that says, "Thora Chamberlain, daughter of a San Jose contractor was seen in Long Beach about 10 a.m."

The telegram is signed, "A Friend, Campbell high school class of 1944."

Thora's not the only child listed as "missing" today in

California. A three-year-old boy, Dickie tum Suden went missing six days ago. Sadly, even as there's new hope today for Thora's rescue, hundreds of soldiers and civilians who have been searching for Dickie near Downieville say they've all but abandoned hope. They've stopped looking for the child, who was last seen in the woods of a mountainous area known as Goodyear's Bar in Sierra County.

Police are considering the possibility that Dickie might have been kidnapped. His maternal grandfather, A. I. Merritt, a gold mine owner, raises that speculation.

However, Dickie's parents have yet to receive a ransom demand. The wealthy socialite couple has more than enough money. So, if the child was abducted, law enforcement authorities are wondering what the kidnappers could be waiting for.

There's speculation -- and someone says they saw -- Dickie being carried off by a mountain lion.

There's also a rumor the child was burned alive, trapped in the basement of the family's mountain cabin when it caught fire.

Four FBI agents are on that case. But there's little hope today that the toddler will be found alive.

While the parents of Thora and Dickie wait minute-by-minute for word that their missing children are okay, there is good news from another missing child case today in California.

Turns out Diana Bickel, like Thora, fourteen years of age, has been found alive and well in the San Francisco home of her grandmother.

Not only did that mysterious telegram concerning Thora lead Sheriff William Emig's men to start looking hard at Long Beach; there's additional evidence that she's alive and well.

This is a break in the case, Emig thinks. True, it's not a cataclysmic, seismic opening, of course. But it's good news, and it gives Emig's team a more substantial lead than they've had to date.

Emig calls a meeting of his deputies.

He says, "A call to the Chamberlain family was placed from Long Beach Tuesday night, the sixth, around 10 p.m. And then another call from Long Beach rang the Chamberlain's phone at nine in the morning yesterday."

One of Emig's deputies asks who was calling, and Emig responds with a shrug, "we don't know. Whoever was calling hung up before the calls were completed.

"We have also discovered that a guy who gave the name "George O'Neill" phoned the telegram to Western Union Tuesday claiming the Chamberlain girl was in Long Beach. And he gave his address as the local YMCA."

The deputies wait expectantly, only to be let down again.

"Unfortunately," Sheriff Emig says, "nobody by that name has stayed at the Y recently."

"So we're right back where we started," mutters one deputy to another.

"But, this gives us hope," Emig assures his men, "new hope."

Meanwhile, the Chamberlain family is taking matters into its own hands.

Thora's parents, Frank and Lois, hand-deliver a statement to local newspapers that is "an earnest appeal to the person responsible for her (Thora's) disappearance to advise us by letter or telephone that she is unharmed."

The parents also ask "all other persons who have any information of any character as to the whereabouts of our daughter to communicate with us" and list their phone number and their home address.

In conclusion, Frank and Lois write, "No one can appreciate the grief and anxiety that have been ours for the past few days. For our sake and the sake of all mothers and fathers, please try to help us in our hour of need."

The family of that missing three-year-old boy in Sierra County can appreciate the Chamberlain's pain only too well.

Not only are the parents of little Dickie tum Suden missing

their child and wondering if he's alive or dead, now they have a new problem.

Once word got out that the search for the toddler was being called off, the family says they began receiving so many crank phone calls they've left their home and moved to what's only described as "an undisclosed location."

Reading the story about Dickie tum Suden's family and their woes on page three of today's San Francisco Examiner, Frank and Lois Chamberlain can only pray it never happens to them.

CHAPTER 12

Six men are waiting for their team leader in the FBI's San Jose, California, office. Dressed exactly the same, each one is in a vested suit, with white shirts, as crisp and freshly laundered as their hair is barbered and faces clean cut.

None of these men would stand out in a crowd, and perhaps that is the point. To a man, they stand between five-foot-six and five-foot-eight inches tall, weighing no more than 165 and no less than 155 pounds. They are trim, lean, and even though they are degreed lawyers and accountants, they are men on a mission.

And, one more thing, unlike most attorneys and bean-counters, each carries a sidearm and is trained to use the crime fighter's favorite weapon, the Thompson submachine gun.

In a few moments, they'll find out what the next mission will be.

The only sound in the room is the soft whirl of a ceiling fan until the conference room's wooden door opens.

At the stroke of 9 a.m., their leader walks into the room.

He's Earl "E. J." Connelley. Born and raised in Columbus, Ohio, E.J. joined the U.S. Army as a private in 1917. Two years later, he was promoted to the rank of first lieutenant.

Once out of the army, E.J. completed his law and accounting studies in New York and joined the FBI as a special agent on January 16, 1920.

By 1927, he was appointed an inspector and rose to the rank of Assistant Director in Charge of Major Investigations in the Field four years after that.

E.J. worked only the FBI's top cases, the most important investigations, as an on-scene supervisor.

E.J. has led these men against some of the nation's most notorious, deadly, and violent gangsters.

Together, they brought down John Dillinger and the mom-and-son team of Ma and Fred Barker.

In response to the abduction of Charles Lindbergh's baby and other high-profile kidnapping cases, Congress passed the Federal Kidnapping Act in 1932. The new law granted authority to the FBI, then known as the Bureau of Investigation, to work kidnapping cases that crossed state lines.

As the years progressed through the 1930s, the FBI would also look for missing children of so-called "tender years," usually thought to be the age of twelve or younger even if the cases didn't cross state boundaries.

However, the FBI's work in kidnapping investigations was not limited to "tender years" nor interstate cases. Agents would also offer assistance to local and state officials when requested.

That moved E.J. and his team into a new arena.

Quick out of the gate, E.J. and his special agents solved the kidnapping-slaying of a retired Chicago businessman, Charles S. Ross.

Then there was the abduction of George Weyerhaeuser, a nine-year-old boy, taken from his family in Tacoma, Washington, on May 24, 1935. His family paid a $200,000 ransom for the boy's return, and eight days after he vanished, George was back in the loving arms of his mother.

But the kidnappers were on the run, constantly looking over their shoulders, with E.J. and this team of special agents in hot pursuit.

The three people who abducted little George made the mistake of spending some of the ransom money. The bills led E.J. and his team to the trio of kidnappers, who would all be arrested and convicted.

E.J also had direct supervision of the Duquesne espionage case that resulted in the arrest and conviction of thirty-three

German agents in 1941-42.

As he stands before his team today, the agents know they won't have to wait long to find out what's on E.J.'s mind. He's just like them, a man on a mission.

Dressed as precisely as his team, E.J. is constantly leaning forward, a razor-thin, intense smile on his face. Yet, there is something that sets him apart.

E.J. has always worn a thin pencil mustache above his upper lip. Despite J. Edgar Hoover's hatred of facial hair, E.J. refuses to shave, and his men love him for that streak of stubbornness.

So, as he walks to the front of the room, the agents each sit straighter, turning their full attention to E. J. Standing before a pulled-down map of the state of California, he begins to speak.

"Gentlemen, another kidnapping case, today; the disappearance of a teenage girl, Thora Chamberlain in Campbell.

"We don't have much to go on, but when has that ever stopped us before?"

The men share a confident chuckle but quickly return to the serious business ahead.

"For days, there has been no sign of Miss Chamberlain. Neighbors, along with her parents, continue to walk the streets of Campbell looking for the girl, but with less enthusiasm and in lesser numbers than the day the child vanished.

"Local police officers, county deputies, and even state police have done what they can.

"Here's what we know so far. Mysterious calls have come into the Chamberlain home. But so far, no ransom demand.

"Her friends say she got into an old blue Plymouth driven by a man dressed in U.S. Navy clothing. A lady named Ella Beaudoux, of Saratoga, tells police about a child matching Thora's description speeding past her in a blue sedan, 'like Dillinger used to drive,' she says.

"But other than those eyewitness accounts, no one has a clue as to the whereabouts of this teenager.

"Gentlemen, this case is going to be a challenge, no doubt about that. But this young girl's friends and family have new hope today because, as of this moment, we are on the case."

CHAPTER 13

The top cop in San Mateo, California, Robert Emmett O'Brien, became the city's second police chief nearly two years ago, February 1, 1944. He moved into the job after his predecessor, Chief Thomas F. Burke, died.

O'Brien's everything E.J. is not, and nothing E.J. is.

Whereas E.J. is built like a whippet, lean, and razor-sharp, with every hair in place on the top of his head, O'Brien's muscular body is hidden by pounds of fat. His hair is wavy, black. It never seems to want to lay still.

And while E.J.'s eyes and face burn with intensity, O'Brien looks like a guy ready to share a beer with buddies and burst into song.

So neither feels like he's looking into a mirror as the two law enforcement men sit across from each other at Chief O'Brien's desk today.

"Good to meet you, Agent Connelley."

"And you as well, Chief O'Brien."

E.J. smiles. He's become accustomed to spending time with local police. They usually solve cases with brawn, not brains. That isn't the way E.J and his men do their jobs.

Still, it is good politics, if nothing else, to give the local cops their due. But E.J. isn't about wasting time either.

"You have information that might help me find Thora Chamberlain's abductor?"

"Well, nothing ironclad." O'Brien pushes an 8X12 inch black-and-white photo toward E.J. "But this is a fellow worth looking at, I think."

E.J. accepts the photo, looks it over once, and sits straight in his wooden chair, waiting for more.

O'Brien leans back in his padded, comfortable leather office swivel chair. He's had a few conversations with the FBI, and while they could be helpful, O'Brien feels they are overgrown college boys who usually just get in the way, what with all their suits, ties, and legal technicalities.

However, this time, he and his local officers are stumped; O'Brien can use all the help the FBI has to offer. He's ready to stop acting like a dog pissing in a circle and let E.J. into his territory.

"That picture you're looking at is a guy by the name of Thomas Henry McMonigle. Thirty-one-years old, an ex-con from Illinois, living with his wife in San Mateo."

"And?"

"And, we can't prove it yet, but we think this McMonigle stole a footlocker from a navy guy. The locker had clothes in it, just like the clothes these friend's of Chamberlain's said the man she drove off with was wearing."

E.J. picks up the black-and-white again. Then he looks across the desk at Chief O'Brien. This is getting interesting.

"McMonigle here," O'Brien says, gesturing at the photo, "has been seen in Campbell. No doubt about that and —"O'Brien pauses to slug back another gulp of lukewarm black coffee.

E.J. waits.

"And," O'Brien moves forward toward E.J., with both forearms on the desk. "And, remember I said he was an ex-convict?"

E.J. would love to tell him to hurry the hell up but sees O'Brien is one of those cops who just loves taking center stage. So instead of pushing, E.J. takes a page from one of the judo courses at the FBI Academy and pulls back from the desk, using the weight of O'Brien's story to pull the facts out of the cop.

"Thomas Henry McMonigle," O'Brien says. E.J. relaxes. He can feel a long monologue coming.

"He is 6 feet 3 inches tall, weighs about 183 pounds, with blue eyes, a ruddy complexion, and a scar on the right side of his forehead, above the eye.

"Born on May 28, 1914, in Covell, McLean County, Illinois — Daddy still lives in Cottage Hill, Illinois, near as we know. Most of his relations are close by. McMonigle is one of eight children.

"This guy's worked as a bus driver, truck driver, and a guard at someplace called Mills Field. Did some boxing, too, when he was a kid. Fought good enough to make the papers in Illinois back when McMonigle was sixteen."

"Any military experience?"

"Not as far as we know. But McMonigle's done plenty of time in a jail cell."

"Oh?"

"Oh yeah. Vagrancy and assault when he was a kid. Minor stuff, but then, there's this. McMonigle did eight-and-a-third years for guess what?"

E.J. raises his hands and eyebrows to make it clear he hasn't a clue.

"Attempted rape, that's what."

Now E.J.'s interest grows. The stolen clothing, if McMonigle did take the footlocker, along with the attempted rape, well, that would give him a higher position on the suspect list.

"When he gets out, McMonigle gets into trouble again. Gets into a fight with his boss at San Mateo Transit Company."

E.J. makes a show of giving O'Brien's story plenty of thought.

O'Brien leans back for more coffee.

"There's this too," O'Brien says. "Back in the spring, the month of May, we ran into him again."

"Oh?" Now it's E.J.'s turn to move forward. He just can't help himself.

"McMonigle was booked into the San Mateo County jail for an alleged assault on a fourteen-year-old girl in San Bruno."

"Fourteen?" Good God, E.J. thinks, the same age as our victim, Thora.

O'Brien takes a deep breath and exhales. It's time for the final shoe to drop, the punchline to this tale of law enforcement woe.

"The only reason he's not doing time for that now is that the girl's family decided not to prosecute. Said they didn't want the publicity and didn't want the girl to have to testify."

"Too bad for Thora," says E.J.

"Yeah," agrees O'Brien. "Too damn bad."

"I just hope, says E.J., "we're in time to save her life."

CHAPTER 14

"We don't have much more to go on yet, but we do have a bit more than we had yesterday," E.J. tells his troops. Again, as yesterday, the only sound aside from agents' pencils scribbling notes on the pads in front of them is the ceiling fan gently whirling in a circle above their heads.

The men are dressed as formally as before. None of them would ever think of showing up to work in anything less than a vested suit, perfectly knotted single-color tie, stiffly starched white shirt, and black shoes that are more than shined; they are polished.

Such an ensemble can be more than a little uncomfortable in the summer. But this time of the year, in this part of California, the temperature never rises above 70-degrees during the day. So the men don't even consider rolling up their sleeves.

However, metaphorically, each has his sleeves rolled up. It's time to go to work.

To begin the meeting, E.J. hands out black-and-white photos of the man he believes might be responsible for Thora's abduction and possible murder.

Then, as his team examines the pictures, E.J. jerks down on the map of California at the front of the room before letting it roll up quickly to reveal what he's written on the blackboard behind.

"First, we have a suspect. A gentleman by the name of Thomas Henry McMonigle," says E.J. He pauses and looks over the heads of the six agents in front of him. Each is bent over the paper pad in front, furiously writing down the name of their suspect.

Even though he has nothing more than O'Brien's hunch and less-than-circumstantial evidence to go on, McMonigle is E.J.'s best suspect at this point. And with the case getting colder by the hour, there's no time to waste.

"We don't have much on him, but we have enough to dig into McMonigle's life first." E.J. waits for the agents' attention to return to him.

"To begin with, you two," he says, pointing at two of him men in the front row, "you are going to find McMonigle and follow him. Go wherever he goes, but of course, don't let him see you."

"What exactly do you mean when you say 'wherever,'" one of the designated agents asks.

"I mean wherever. You have a car. Use it if you have to. We have bureau expense accounts, too, so don't be afraid to follow his man wherever he goes. Wherever."

The men nod their understanding, copy off more information E.J. has written on the blackboard, and move off into a corner to compare notes and develop a plan of action.

"And you two," E.J. says nodding at another pair off agents, "you are to go to McMonigle's place of employment." E.J. points to the lines of the blackboard listing the company name and address of the construction company in Burlingame.

"We also need to talk to the young lady in San Bruno who accused McMonigle of assaulting her. We need to speak to her parents as well. Harris and Edwards, you take that assignment."

"Think they'll want to talk this time?" The agent who's asked the pointed query lays down his pencil. None of the men has ever had a problem asking questions of E.J. after all of the cases they've worked together. It's more than a feeling of shared respect and admiration; they've developed a bond that few have in the FBI.

E.J. fixes him with the eyes of an eagle. His smile is tight as he says, "Well, I guess it's going to be your job to convince them to talk."

And then, to answer the question on everyone's mind, as E.J. picks up his photo of McMonigle, he says, "And my job? I am going to talk to Thora's friends; these girls may have been the last people to see her alive."

CHAPTER 15

E.J. crosses his legs, smiles gently, and tries to put the three young girls in front of him at ease. He thinks they ought to be at home listening to songs on the radio like 'Sentimental Journey.' Or maybe they'd rather be at the corner soda shop talking about boys and listening to Perry Como sing, 'Till the End of Time' on the jukebox.

If nothing else, these teenage girls — and everyone else in Campbell for that matter — should be celebrating the end of World War Two and moving on with their lives.

Instead, parents worry constantly about their daughters, praying they never go missing as Thora has.

Girls like the five in front of him might seem cavalier. But behind their bobbysoxer bravado, E.J. knows they were also only too aware of what happened to one of their own.

If nothing else, these three — 16-year-old Elaine Scimeca and her friends — should be anywhere else but the Campbell High School principal's office, meeting with the FBI agent who solved numerous gangster kidnappings and helped put John Dillinger in a grave.

But, here they are.

"Tell me," E.J. says, "what were you all doing the afternoon of November second?"

The girls look at each other, not sure who should speak first or what they should say. If nothing else, they couldn't agree more with E.J. on one point — besides the initial excitement, they would love to be doing anything else but talking to the FBI.

E.J. relaxes, and his smile becomes broader. "You were all

going to a football game, right?"

"That's correct, sir," says Elaine. "All of us were together."

"And Thora too," says Catherine.

"Fine. What happened while you were walking to the game?"

The girls quickly repeat the story they'd told more times than they could remember. They talk about the man in a blue car pulling up alongside them as they walked on Winchester.

Rita tells E.J. and her friends nod in agreement, how the man in the car said he needed someone to babysit his sister's kids.

And then finally, with a sigh, Elaine and Catherine, completing each other's sentences, tell the story of how Thora got in the car and drove away.

"Good job," E.J. says. He leans forward and meets each girl's eyes in turn. "Now, tell me, what do you remember this man was wearing."

Unfortunately, none of the girls say they got close enough to see much, but Rita remembers a white Navy t-shirt with medals pinned on it. The other girls nod their agreement. Each had seen enough returning naval personnel to immediately recognize the shirt.

E.J. nods and opens a folder he's been carrying. He takes out seven black-and-white photos of men with black hair. All are about the same age, in their early thirties. And each is smiling.

"I need you to tell me if you remember seeing any of these men that day, November second."

The girls each take a deep breath. They're more comfortable now, almost feeling like they're in a movie. Looking at photos of suspects. This is what always happens; the girls think as one.

They go through the pictures once, twice, and finally a third time.

One by one, the girls each point at the same photo.

Five of the photos were taken of police officers. The sixth and the one selected by the girls is that of Thomas Henry McMonigle.

CHAPTER 16

It's an early morning for agents Fred R. Elledge and Michael H. Farrin. They're drinking lukewarm coffee from a couple of pre-war thermoses they purchased from some ex-GI Joes looking to make a quick buck.

The agents got on the road early today. Driving north about thirty miles along the eastern side of the peninsula toward San Francisco. Their task is to interview the guys who work with Thomas McMonigle at the construction yard in Burlingame.

Neither agent was overjoyed or even pleased to be on the road at 6 a.m. They're not feeling much better now.

"We gotta be there before 8 a.m. before these guys punch in. Otherwise, nobody, even if they want to talk to us, will be able to take time for a conversation," Farrin says over the complaints still being voiced by Elledge.

They make it. Bucked the early morning traffic, which is becoming an absolute nightmare, in Burlingame, what with the factories going full-tilt as they are converted from wartime to peacetime manufacturing.

It was never a secret that California's factories were getting one-eighth of all military manufacturing orders during the war. So millions of Americans who weren't in uniform came to California to do their part and make a nice living at the same time.

As a result, roads and highways built for six-million people are jammed with cars and trucks driven by millions more.

Still, Farrin and Elledge make it to Burlingame and park outside the yard before most of Thomas's co-workers arrive.

When the employees start showing up, most often in pairs sharing rides, the agents get out of their car, toss the now-cold coffee onto the sandy ground, flip their cigarette butts the way only a seasoned smoker does, and walk toward the first group of workers.

Neither Elledge nor Farrin need to show their FBI badges — it's like they've got the words 'Law Enforcement' tattooed on their foreheads. Besides, who but a cop would show up at a construction yard in a vested suit wearing a tie and polished shoes.

But the agents flip open their ID cases anyway. Damn it, they're proud to be agents and have been doing it long enough to know the weight an FBI badge carries.

"We need to talk about one of your buddies," says Elledge as he's approached by a couple of guys who look like the redwoods that grow in California's forests.

None of the construction workers responds to Elledge's statement, so Farrin adds, "We think he's been playing around with little girls. Children. Any idea who we want to talk about?"

Since they are close to half a foot shorter than the construction workers and face the east, the FBI agents are forced to look up and squint into the morning sunrise.

Construction workers, must be six or seven of them, move a few steps forward and surround the agents. But instead of looking threatening, the workers share looks with each other, waiting to be the first to speak.

"I think they know who we're looking for, Agent Farrin," says Elledge. Damn the sun, he thinks and blinks away a tear caused by the blinding sunlight.

"Question is, Agent Farrin, do they all play together?"

That was all it took. The workers start talking and can't stop.

"McMonigle," says one worker.

The others nod.

"Thomas Henry McMonigle, right?"

"He's trouble," says another worker. He looks at Farrin, begging him with his eyes to ask the obvious follow-up question,

The seasoned agent reads his mind and plays along.

"What kind of trouble?

"We haven't seen Thomas for days," says a new member of the group. He's smaller than the others, but he's still a giant compared to former accountants Elledge and Farrin, with arms that could bend steel bars.

Silence.

Then, Farrin says, "Again, gentlemen, I ask; what kind of trouble?"

"Like we said," answers the worker, "Thomas ain't been here since the beginning of the month."

"November 6," says another new member of the gallery. This guy's holding a clipboard. Elledge pegs him for a foreman or at least an office worker.

"Yeah," says one of the first employees on the scene. "Worked hard that day, he did. Built that little bridge and ramp over there."

"Doesn't sound like he was much trouble," says Farrin.

More nervous glances. The workers know what has to be said but can't decide who's going to say it.

Finally, the biggest of the crew speaks up.

"Few days before he took a powder, Thomas came to work bragging about where he'd been."

"Yeah?" Farrin says. Elledge moves closer to the big guy.

The big guy licks his lips and looks to his buddies for support.

"He'd been missing for about a week," says another worker.

"That's right," the giant among his fellow-men says, "and then he shows up out of nowhere. We ask where the hell he'd been."

Silence.

"And," Farrin says. "Where had he been?"

The big guy takes a deep breath. Two of the others push him a step closer to agents Elledge and Farrin.

The big guy looks down at them and says, "Thomas told us he'd been with a fifteen-year-old girl."

The workers all nod their agreement. And two or three offer verbal assurances that the big guy's telling the truth.

"Jesus," Farrin whispers and looks at his partner for further comment. Elledge remains silent.

For a moment, he's forgotten how to breathe.

CHAPTER 17

Neither FBI agent Harris nor agent Edwards speaks a word. It's like radio silence has been in effect since they threw themselves into an agency-issued Ford and drove to Andrea Dyson's San Bruno home.

Sullen, depressed and angry. The two men are all three. But they're also excited. Neither wants to believe what they'd just heard.

Finally, Harris yanks his beat-up grey fedora off his head and tosses it on the dashboard. Edwards glances at him from behind the steering wheel as he pushes the car into third gear.

Harris meets Edwards' glance.

"Why do you think EJ picked us for this job?"

"How the hell should I know?"

Harris clicks on the radio. At least they had what passed for a new car, a 1942 Ford Super Deluxe Tudor Sedan. It was the last of the vehicles that rolled off Ford's assembly lines for the general public before Henry's kin converted everything to military production. Even this car has a hint of what was to come — no chrome. Instead, where the chrome should have been, only silver paint.

But the Tudor Sedan Harris and Edwards are riding in through San Bruno has the latest of everything, including a radio, along with a circle speedometer and a clock.

Harris cranks up the radio's volume just before Edwards uses another spiffy new feature in the Tudor, a floor button that he can touch with his foot to shut off the radio.

"No, I'm not kidding," says Harris as he cedes the battle of the radio to his partner for the day. "Why the fuck did we get the job of talking to some poor kid who got raped by this perv?"

Edwards answers, "Luck of the draw? Short stick? Don't have a clue, friend. It's above my pay grade."

They know they're heading for a rough session at the Dyson family home. Neither Andrea nor her parents want to talk about what had happened to the child. They only agreed to the coming conversation because of the weight of the letters "FBI."

Finding the house is easy. Getting themselves out of the Ford and onto the front porch is another story.

Brief introductions, Mrs. Dyson, offers coffee and cookies; Edwards and Harris accept.

Then the conversation begins.

Just as the agents hoped and EJ predicted, Andrea picks McMonigle's 8X10 out of a stack of black-and-white photos.

But that turns out to be just the beginning.

Then, the girl takes a deep breath, closes her eyes, and tells Harris and Edwards about how McMonigle had pulled up alongside her as she was walking to school.

"He told me his sister needed a babysitter," Andrea says.

Both of the agents sit up straighter. The parents might be all weepy, but this fifteen-year-old kid, with a maturity beyond her years, tells the story Edwards and Harris need to hear.

"Oh yeah, and what then?" Harris asks.

Andrea sniffs back some tears, wipes her eyes with Edwards's handkerchief, and gets ready to continue.

This kid's got some moxie, Edwards thinks as he notices Daddy looks like he wants his little girl to stay quiet.

Harris notices the same thing and shuts down Papa Dyson with a stern look.

"Go ahead," Edwards whispers.

Andrea keeps talking like Mommy and Daddy aren't even there.

"So I get in the car." She looks up at Edwards. "He was going to pay me a fiver, at least that's what he said."

Andrea throws a quick look at Harris and then refocuses on Edwards.

"You can buy a lot of stuff with five bucks."

Edwards nods. He doesn't say a word. The last thing he wants to do is to give Andrea a reason to stop talking.

Harris is watching the Mister and Missus. They holding hands, tears running down their cheeks. It's tugging at Harris's heartstrings too. But like Edwards, he doesn't want to stop the momentum. Andrea needs to tell this story.

Do the parents need to hear it? Who knows, thinks Edwards. These two aren't a couple of geezers, but they are getting older by the minute.

Better finish this as fast as possible.

"So —"Andrea says and waits.

"So," says Edwards, trying to prompt her to keep talking by raising his eyebrows to let the kid know he's all ears.

"So," Andrea says with a sigh. "I get into his car. It was blue, a Plymouth," she says. Andrea's been asked to describe the car so many times, she repeats the color and model by rote.

"And?"

"And, we start driving," Andrea says. "And we're driving and driving. All of a sudden, I realize we are not in San Bruno anymore."

"Where were you?"

"Going across the Peninsula. Toward Devil's Slide. I start to panic. Went a little crazy. I grabbed the door handle and pulled it. Ready to jump, I was."

Andrea's breathing so fast. Edwards and Harris are afraid she's going to pass out. They're wondering if Mom has a spare paper bag just in case Andrea starts hyperventilating.

"He grabs for me, gets my arm, and pulls me back. Then he drives to the side, hits the skids. I look in his eyes, and he is so angry."

Andrea's not the only one breathing fast right now. Her parents are inhaling and exhaling like a couple of marathon runners.

Edwards and Harris, meanwhile, are doing their best to remember how to breathe. EJ is going to flip when he hears this tale, both think.

"Then he lets me go and opens the glovebox. But as soon as he lets go, I grab the door handle, and the door opens. I jump out and run.

"He came right after me. I didn't get far. He tackled me, jumped on me, and — "

After a few moments of silence, Edwards says what needs saying.

"And?"

"And he puts a gun to my head and does what he did. Then after a while, we hear a car, and he just runs off."

Andrea walks over to the sofa where her parents have melted in tears and collapses between mom and dad.

No one says a word.

Edwards and Harris lean back in their kitchen chairs. But in the next heartbeat, both men look around the room and realize the past thirty minutes are among the most grueling half-hours the Dyson family will ever face.

So without a goodbye, Edwards and Harris mash their fedoras on their heads, make sure they've left their cards, and show themselves out.

Good God, both men think. EJ is going to flip when he hears this.

CHAPTER 18

Lou Wilson and Ken Ridell push their way inside when Ena opens the front door a crack.

Wilson flashes his FBI badge and is pleased to see Ena blanch at the sight of the federal ID. But he and his partner also take note of how quickly she recovers from her initial shock.

"Thomas McMonigle," says Wilson.

"Yeah?"

"He here?" Ridell moves within inches of Ena, but she doesn't step back.

"Well?" Wilson says. He, too, moves into Ena's space. But again, instead of retreating, Ena defiantly lifts her chin into the air.

"Listen, Ena, you know who we are, don't you?" Ridell says.

"We aren't just a couple of local cops. We're feds, and we can rain a ton of shit down on your parade." Wilson says.

"So come clean. We know you and McMonigle are married. Is he in this house or not?"

"Maybe we should just tear it apart," Ridell says.

Now, Ena backs down. With shoulders and chin lowered, she looks down to the floor then back up to the agents.

"He ain't here. That's the honest truth. Tommy said he was going to L.A.," Ena says. "That's all I know."

"Oh come on, sister, You're his wife," says Wilson. "You let him out of here without knowing where he was going in Los Angeles?"

Ridell taps Ena on the shoulder both to get her attention and reinforce the dominant position taken by him and Wilson.

"Driving?"

Ena shakes her head and points at the car keys on the coffee table.

"Tossed me the keys to the Plymouth, said he was going to take the bus, and left. That's all I know."

"When's he coming back?"

Again Ena shrugs.

Wilson looks at Ridell, and silently, they agree.

"Ena, honey, we're going to take a quick look around just to be sure you're telling the truth," Wilson says

Ridell adds, "You sure there's nothing else you want to tell us?"

After Ena shakes her head, Ridell and Wilson pull their service revolvers out and do a quick search of the tiny house with guns in hand. Doesn't take long to convince themselves that Thomas has flown the coop.

Ridell drops an FBI business card on the coffee table and grabs the car keys as he and Wilson move quickly to the front door.

"He shows up again, you call us, understand?"

With that, two more men walk out of Ena's life. She looks over her shoulder, catching her breath. Not much more to do now but clean up the messes all three men left behind.

Then she sees a police department tow truck in the driveway hooking up to Thomas's Plymouth. Ena sighs. Looks like she'll be riding the bus for a while.

With Wilson behind the wheel, the agents race to the closest bus stop, as quickly as their FBI Ford will take them. Hopping out of the car almost before it stops, Ridell talks to a couple of lost souls waiting for the next bus. A couple of teenage girls, bobbysoxers. Funny enough, they actually remember Thomas.

"Yeah, he was funny," says one of the women.

"Cute too," giggles the other. "Dreamboat!"

Ridell fixes the girls with his coldest stare. But they're too young to be impressed by much. So he has to wait for the girls to calm down.

"Got on a bus to Los Angeles?" Wilson says after joining the party.

He takes down the girls' names and addresses, phone numbers too, while Ridell drops a nickel into a payphone to report back to E.J.

After a quick conversation, he moves back toward Wilson.

"And?" Wilson says, knowing what the answer will be.

"We're off to Los Angeles," says Ridell. "The chase is on.'

CHAPTER 19

Agents Lou Wilson and Ken Ridell race toward Los Angeles. They don't have a siren in their car, no bubble gum lights, so they are fated to go not much faster than traffic flow. "Damn," says Wilson, "this is one of those days where everyone driving faster than you is a knucklehead and cars going too slow are Sunday drivers."

"Sure, it would be nice to have one of the local black-and-whites," Ridell says, missing his partner's sarcasm. He drums his fingers on the steering wheel as he and Wilson wait for the slowest traffic light in history to blink from red to green.

But, fortunately, at this time of night, even California slows down some until, of course, they get into L.A.

Here, it's a madhouse, a city with no limits, almost no law, a frontier town of returning GIs who are just happy to be home alive and in nearly one piece.

The agents find their way to the main L.A. bus terminal, and Ridell jumps out of the Ford as Wilson searches for a parking spot.

The inside of the terminal is as wild as the heart of Los Angeles. People drink alcohol with abandoned, chugging bottles of booze like there's no tomorrow.

Couples are making out in the dark corners of the terminal's main floor, kissing, petting, groping, and some are going all the way. It could be a few call-girls making some moolah, but Ridell thinks not.

Is it New Year's Eve already, Wilson wonders? Or did I wander into Sodom and Gomorrah?

He sees Ridell pushing his way through the crowd.

"Madness, huh?" Ridell says.

Wilson's out of breath, his fedora is jammed flat on his head after he rescued his hat from a couple of hipster dollies who have a problem with authority.

"Where is he? Goddamn, how the hell are we going to find McMonigle in this zoo?"

Ridell shrugs his shoulders and looks around. Then, over Wilson's shoulder, he sees the answer.

"Cast your peepers over yonder partner, what do you see?

Wilson spins a 180-degree turn at Ridell's behest, and a smile slowly cuts through the 8 o'clock shadow clouding his jaw.

Both men are transfixed more than any adult male should be by the sight of at least ten, maybe fifteen, young girls. None of them are older than sixteen, so none of them are old enough to smoke the Pall Malls being passed around. A couple of the baby dolls wear jeans. Most of the others wear Shetland sweaters, and Wilson spots a couple of those poodle skirts in the crowd.

However, what the girls all have in common when it comes to fashion is they are all wearing either penny loafers or saddle shoes and bobby sox.

"Just the kind of girls our man would love," Ridell says. Wilson doesn't hear a word of that; he's already moving through the crowd toward the young ladies.

Ridell knocks a couple of juvie knuckleheads out of his way and moves alongside his partner.

"Hey, look at the flat-foots," shouts the bravest of the young bobbysoxers.

A quick look from Ridell and a flash of Wilson's FBI badge shocks her into silence as one of her friends, with wide-eyed amazement whispers, "Hot damn, it's a G-man."

"That's correct little lady," Wilson says while Ridell snatches the cigarette out of the mouth of the girl who'd insulted the condition of his arches.

"We need some help."

The girls push forward.

Wilson pulls an 8X10 of Thomas out of his suit coat pocket and shows it to the girls. "Any of you see this guy around tonight?"

The teenagers whisper and giggle again. Finally, a consensus is reached, and a brave female soul steps forward.

Ridell wonders if she smuggled those blue jeans she's wearing out of her house. Her parents couldn't have let her go out in public like this, he decides.

But Wilson doesn't give it a thought. To him, the blue jeans just show this girl is going to speak her mind.

She takes a deep breath and looks up at Wilson with the sweetest blue eyes he's ever seen. She's an authentic dish.

"You gotta name?"

"Yeah," she tells Wilson. She looks at her friends before looking back at him.

"Call me, Diane."

"Okay, Diane, have any of you ever seen this guy?'

The girls giggle again, and one makes like she's going to faint.

"That's Thomas," says Diane.

"He's a dreamboat," says another girl.

"Or at least that's what he thinks," chimes in a third.

Wilson and Ridell look at each other. Just like at the bus stop in San Mateo. Thomas likes these girls more than he should and the girls kind of go for him too.

And right now, Wilson and Ridell are liking Thomas more than ever for the abduction of one, Thora Chamberlain.

"Still here?" Not much of a chance of that, but Wilson can always hope.

"Oh no," says a girl wearing a Shetland sweater, standing in the back of the pack, "he wanted one of us to go with him to babysit his sister's kid."

"But nobody wanted to, so he hit the road," says another.

"You mean he hopped on another bus?"

"Nope," Diane tells Wilson. "He just took off outside, started walking down the road."

Wilson and Ridell know what that means; Thomas is hitching

a ride.

They start running back to their car, which of course, is parked about a mile away.

"Thanks, girls," Wilson shouts over his shoulder.

A few of the girls wave. The rest, well, they do what bobbysoxers do; they giggle and whisper amongst themselves.

Wilson runs to the car while Ridell stops at a kiosk to grab a phone and call EJ.

Ridell isn't embarrassed to have lost their prime suspect. But he isn't overjoyed to have to fess up either.

He doesn't waste time with a "hello," or "how are you?"

Ridell gets right to the point.

"He's vanished, boss."

Ridell only nods in response to EJ's side of the conversation, then slams the receiver back in place before running back to Wilson.

"Where to?"

Ridell opens the driver's side door as Wilson does the same on the other side of the car.

"Back to HQ," Ridell says. "E.J.'s mounting a full-scale operation. No way McMonigle is going to stay disappeared for long."

CHAPTER 20

November 20, 1945

Harry Truman's making news again today. The president thinks the nation needs a national health care insurance program. Republicans say that would be nothing but socialized medicine.

Agents have no time to read the story unless they grab a paper and head down the hall to the men's room. Nobody's taken much of a break since McMonigle vanished.

Only a couple of days until Thanksgiving, but baring a holiday miracle, nobody on E.J.'s team expects more than warmed-over turkey and cold cranberry sauce this year.

There will be no rest until Thomas McMonigle is arrested and Thora Chamberlain rescued.

As soon as E.J. got the word that Thomas had vanished, he started dialing other FBI offices in the West and Midwest.

Special Agents in Charge rallied to his cause. Thomas is now a wanted man, and he very well could have a child with him, Thora Chamberlain.

If true, Thomas is taking Thora across state lines. That makes this a federal case.

Ridell and Wilson are soon not alone. A team of thirty FBI agents is quickly assembled, and they will be spending their days and nights searching for Thomas Henry McMonigle, and of course, Thora Chamberlain.

Everything and everyone is in place. Still, the attitude in E.J.'s home office is more than anxious as he waits for word from his men in the field.

Finally, the phone rings.

"Boss, we've got a tip. McMonigle's been seen in Cottage Hills, Illinois. A civilian spotted him."

E.J. leaps to his feet and moves quickly from behind his oak desk. The tip's just a tip, but it makes sense. McMonigle's family lives in that area. That's why E.J. called his colleagues in the Midwest for assistance. His hunch could be paying off.

Still, two simple questions are at the front of his mind.

"When and where?"

"The post office," the agent on the phone answers. "A Joe Citizen thinks he saw him picking up mail."

Damn. This could be the break we need, E.J. thinks.

Of course, citizens can always make mistakes, agents too. No identification is every ironclad until we get the fingerprints, he's fond of saying.

But that doesn't mean E.J. is going to hesitate.

"This is the biggest break we've had since McMonigle vanished from California. So let's move on it," E.J. orders.

In a few hours, more information comes in from Illinois. Agents on the ground confirm the rumor.

"This is Thomas McMonigle," one of them whispers excitedly down the line to the San Jose office. "We've got him."

The agent answering the call holds the receiver away from his ear so E.J. can listen to the conversation.

His patience wearing thin, E.J. grabs the receiver and says sternly, "Don't any of you get too close. We know he beat up his boss once, and he did a lot of boxing as a youth.

"Remember, this guy could be violent, and he knows how to handle himself."

E.J. waits for the agent in Illinois to grunt his understanding. But at the same time, E.J. knows the agent is only half-listening. He's chomping at the bit, ready to make the arrest.

E.J. knows the feeling. The agents who've spotted McMonigle are like hounds who've seen the fox. They have more than the scent of their prey in their nostrils.

They have seen him up close and personal.

So E.J. cautions the agent again to hold his ground and his water.

"The most important reason to hold back is that McMonigle could still have Thora Chamberlain, the girl we think he kidnapped. Get too close, and he might harm her. Or worse. So stay back."

With those instructions delivered, E.J. hangs up the receiver, then picks it up quickly. He begins dialing the number of the Special Agent in Charge in Chicago.

Theoretically, both men are equal in rank. But E.J. is in charge of this investigation, and more importantly, his reputation for solving these abduction cases supersedes any bureaucratic notions of rank.

"I want the thirty agents we have in the field moved to Cottage Hills, Illinois. Their number-one job is to track McMonigle's every move," E.J. says. "If he's in a car, I want two agents trailing him in their autos."

The connection's a little bit scratchy, but E.J. knows a pencil is scribbling notes on the other end of the line. He waits for the agent to catch up.

"Tell those guys not to forget they've got two-way radios in their cars. Keep in touch. We don't want any heroes here. Make sure all the agents know what each other is doing."

More scratching and scribbling.

"If McMonigle goes into a bar, make sure there are agents outside waiting for him. And we need to have a team always undercover too. I don't want this guy vanishing through a bathroom window."

There must be an undercover team in every bar or restaurant McMonigle visits.

"Wherever he goes, we need to have two undercover agents with him at all times. And make sure they keep their walkie-talkies nearby and use them for Pete's sake."

"What about if he goes into a relative's house or a friend's house?" The agent on the other end says, "We know McMonigle's got at least four family members in two houses in Cottage Hills."

"Obviously, we can't send an undercover into the houses," says E.J. "But there's got to be a car with two agents parked outside. And the undercover agents — don't send them inside, but put them in the neighborhood watching the rear of the house."

E.J. pauses to wait for the sounds of scribbling to stop. He also wants to make sure he hasn't forgotten anything.

"And, this is most important," E.J. says just as the other agent figures their conversation had come to a conclusion.

"We've only got thirty agents on this case," says E.J. "I know that sounds like plenty, but these guys are going to be constantly on McMonigle's tail, and he's no dummy.

"Make sure our guys work in shifts. Scramble it up. No telling how long this will go on. We don't need McMonigle recognizing our guys and figuring out we're tailing him.

"I do not want McMonigle vanishing again, and most importantly, I don't want him going crazy and doing anything to the girl."

CHAPTER 21

November 23, 1945

America celebrated President Harry Truman's "day of national thanksgiving" on November 22; Thomas McMonigle and his family were no exception.

Today, Thomas is on the move. He stops at his father's house at 316 Goulding Avenue in East Alton. Then he hopscotches from one home to the other, visiting four family members in the Cottage Hills area.

Yet, when one of Thomas's relatives drives him to his sister Alma's home in Alton, Illinois, where he plans to spend the night, Alma says she's not happy.

Alma knows something is wrong.

"The whole family can tell something's amiss," she tells a neighbor. "We're just waiting for something to happen."

Alma might be tense, but Thomas doesn't seem to have a worry on his mind. He's doing nothing but having the time of his life this holiday week.

For instance, he leads the FBI on one wild chase after another. Along the way, Thomas visits as many bars as he can find, hopping from one tavern to the next in most of Alton's neighborhoods.

And Thomas makes friends along the way.

"You need a place to stay tonight? No problem, buddy," says one of his new drinking pals. "Nah, my wife won't complain much."

So, at closing time, Thomas and his new best friend walk off arm-in-arm. Guess who's not far behind. That's right. The FBI.

Two undercover agents, pretending they've had as much to drink as Thomas and his friend, stumble along about a block behind the pair.

At the same time, a nondescript car slowly crawls a block behind the FBI undercover agents. It will soon speed up and park across the street from where Thomas will spend the night.

The strolling agents walk down the boulevard as another team parks behind the house where Thomas will sleep off the night's fun.

The next night, Thomas is in a cab that suddenly rockets off at a high rate of speed, charting a zig-zag course through narrow city streets. It's obvious to the FBI that he's trying to shake them.

Later, after he gets out of the cab and goes into yet another bar, a pair of FBI agents stops the yellow vehicle and grills the driver.

"Yeah, I know, Thomas," the cabbie says. "Everybody knows him in this town."

The cab driver is shaken but hardly overwhelmed by the G-men with their FBI badges. This isn't the first time he's been grilled by a group of lawmen.

"The local cops have been asking all of us cabbies about Thomas," the cab driver says. "We know something's up, but none of us had any idea you G-men were on the case."

One of the agents says, "What about your buddy, McMonigle? Is he aware that we're in town?"

The cabbie lights up another Chesterfield and says, "Of course he doesn't know. What do you think?"

The cab driver, who looks like he could go a few rounds with Thomas and any of the FBI agents, peers through a cloud of cigarette smoke.

"He knows the Alton police have been asking around about him, and yeah, Thomas is a little nervous."

"Well, let's keep this our little secret," says another of the agents.

Breaking off the conversation, one of the FBI team gets on

his walkie-talkie to advise another team of federal agents that Thomas knows he's being followed.

"Got it," says the team leader parked outside Alma's house. He sees Thomas getting out of a cab before stumbling up the walk to the front door.

"We'll put him to bed tonight and keep a close eye on Mr. McMonigle," says the agent. "He won't go anywhere without us. I guarantee it."

CHAPTER 22

November 24, 1945

Thomas leaves Alma's house and walks to the train station. The FBI team that parked for the night outside his sister's residence has been replaced by a couple of new, well-rested agents.

Once Thomas has walked a block away from Alma's one of the G-men, casually dressed, gets out of the car, and starts strolling behind him.

The other agent stays in the car and picks up a walkie-talkie to advise another carload of agents behind the house that Thomas is on the move.

There's a real swagger in Thomas's step today as he bounces along the sidewalk heading downtown for the train station. Once there, he buys a ticket and hops on an Alton Railroad train bound for Springfield, Illinois.

Two of the FBI agents get on the train, as well, while their partners drive on to Springfield.

Once the train stops in Springfield, Thomas gets off the train at 2 p.m. and gets into one of cabs idling by the train station waiting for passengers.

There's already another passenger in the cab, but he's more than willing to share the ride with Thomas.

"Sure, hop in," says the man in the backseat of the Yellow Cab. "No problem. We share the ride and the fare?"

"That works for me," says Thomas as he slides into the backseat of the cab and extends his right hand to make yet another new friend.

"Where to?" says the cab driver.

Thomas tells the driver to head for Springfield, as his buddy in the back seat says that's where he's going, too.

"Small world," Thomas's fellow traveler says. As he smiles and settles back for the ride to Springfield, a Ford four-door pulls out onto the street, staying two car lengths behind the cab.

The miles fly by as the two new best friends talk about their lives. They pull into Springfield, Illinois and Thomas tells the cabbie to stop at a hotel.

"I gotta make a phone call," Thomas explains. "After that, we'll keep going."

The cabbie pulls over to the curb, and before his traveling buddy can react, Thomas jumps from the cab and slams the door shut.

With his riding companion in the cab, who will be stuck for the fare, struggling to get out of the cab, Thomas hails a second cab and drives off.

"Take me to Jacksonville," Thomas says from the backseat as the taxi driver pulls down the lever that starts the car's meter running.

Thomas leans back in the seat and looks out the rear window. The car following the first cab is parked, and the guy who was riding with Thomas is shouting into a walkie-talkie, while the cabbie is obviously demanding payment from two men wearing lookalike suits.

Thomas chuckles to himself, "Don't those rummies think I know what a G-man looks like?'

CHAPTER 23

Thomas is heading for Jacksonville. And, of course, the FBI is in hot pursuit. The agents are traveling close to the cab. Only a couple of car lengths behind.

"Damn, it," says the agent in the passenger seat of the two-door Ford Coupe, "he's going to spot us."

"Not a chance," replies the driver. 'We are not too close. Besides, even if we were, McMonigle doesn't have the rearview. The cabbie can see us, but what does he care?"

Exasperated, the agent in the passenger seat, junior of the pair of law enforcers, scrunches down, jamming his fedora onto his head. The brim's over his eyes. At least this way, the younger agent thinks, McMonigle might not recognize me.

Unbeknownst to the agents in the Ford, they are far down Thomas's list of problems, at least at this moment.

Turns out he's flat broke. Busted. Not a penny to his name, and rather than risk a beating by surprising the taxi driver with the emptiness of his pockets in Jacksonville, Thomas comes clean from the back seat.

"You son of a bitch," says the cabbie, who is far less understanding than Thomas had hoped.

The cab comes to a skidding halt, which forces the FBI man at the wheel of the Ford to make a quick decision. Two choices. Stop or keep going.

If he stops, it will be only too obvious they are tailing Thomas. If he goes around the cab and drives on, the agents risk losing their prey.

"Just keep driving," yells the passenger to his senior agent.

"We can pull up around that curve and hideout."

"Good thinking," says the driver, "we'll be able to keep an eye on him."

"And that's all we want."

"Yeah, and it would be damn nice if McMonigle leads us to that girl."

"That's all we can hope for," says his younger partner.

So the agents round a curve ahead of the cab and wait.

Inside the Yellow Cab, McMonigle's doing his best to work his magic on the cab driver with one of those Semper Fidelis Marine Corps tattoos on his left forearm.

And the tattoo bounces as the cab driver squeezes his hand into a fist.

"Listen," says Thomas, "there's no reason to go crazy. I don't have cash, that's true. But I do have this."

Thomas reaches into a small leather bag he's using to carry his essentials and pulls out an electric razor.

The cab driver raises his eyebrows.

"Look here. It's a brand-new, right out-of-the-box Remington. One of the new Rands," Thomas declares. "Get me to Jacksonville, and it's yours."

The cabbie throws open his drivers' side door, so hard Thomas is afraid it's going to fall off its hinges. With the same force, the cab driver rips open the backseat door and pulls Thomas out of the cab.

Now, Thomas is no lightweight, and he could hold his own in a tussle with this guy. Thomas, however, is also smart enough to know the last thing he needs is to get busted for fighting, so he backs off.

Thomas takes a few steps backward as the cabbie comes at him.

His hands raised in a sign of surrender, Thomas gets ready to dodge the first punch. If he has to fight, he will, but he'd rather not.

The cab driver throws a left at his flat-broke passenger. When Thomas dodges the jab, the ex-Marine uses his right hand to grab the Remington away from Thomas.

The cabbie looks at the razor, thinks about the shave he's needed for two days at least, and glares at Thomas. Not another word is spoken between the men.

The cab driver gets back in his car and drives off, thinking Thomas is damn lucky he didn't throw a punch.

And Thomas is thinking the same thing as he trudges up the road. "I could have killed that mug," Thomas grumbles.

After a few steps, Thomas begins ambling backward with his thumb thrust out in the universal sign of one who needs a lift.

And does he ever need a ride. Thomas can't remember the last authentic meal he's had. Probably hasn't had three squares since Alma served dinner a couple of nights ago.

Now he's walking, and there's nothing until a bit of burg called Quincy miles ahead.

Thomas looks down at his thumb and smirks. What the hell am I doing? There isn't a car for miles.

So, it's either hoof it or lay down for a nap. Thomas is going back and forth in his mind, weighing the alternatives, when out of nowhere, a two-door Ford slows and stops.

Thomas is so lost in thought it seems like the car dropped out of the sky. Could this be one of those mirages he's read about?

"Need a lift? Where are you going?"

There are two guys in the front seat of the Ford. The inquisitive one is in the passenger seat. He hops out and, with the door open, invites Thomas to sit between him and the driver.

Thomas hesitates only slightly. These guys look legit. No doubt they're a couple of vacuum cleaner salesmen. Or maybe they're selling Bibles.

Thomas, at the moment, doesn't care. And, he's changed his mind about his destination.

"Quincy," he says, making himself comfortable between his new best friends. "I'm going to Quincy. Thanks, fellas."

CHAPTER 24

The two guys in the Ford and Thomas have a jolly time driving to Quincy. After dropping him off, where else, at a bar — the two go around the corner and park behind a row of buildings.

Then, on their two-way, the FBI agents call out to their Quincy brothers-in-blue. After a quick radio conversation, two local undercover cops meet Thomas in the bar.

"I'm dead broke," Thomas tells the pair as he begs with his puppy-dog eyes for one more Boilermaker — a shot of whiskey and a beer. Only too glad to oblige, the team sits like bookends at Thomas's left and right.

"If you're willing to work," says one of the police officers, who winks at the barmaid to let her know he is on duty, "I know a couple of factories that are hiring."

"And," says his buddy, "we know the guys to talk to about getting a job."

Thomas pauses to slug down the shot of whiskey and takes a long drink of beer.

"Hard work?"

"Yeah, well, it's not easy, or anybody could do it," answers the first undercover officer.

"That's why they pay good," says his friend parked on Thomas's left. "And you get cash at the end of every day."

Well, cash would be Thomas's second-best friend right now, second only to this pair of local yokels who don't mind keeping the bar's beer tap — and their wallets —open.

"The local telegraph office is hiring too," says the barmaid, who is only too happy to join the conversation.

That's all Thomas needs to know. His thirst quenched, Thomas leaves the bar with his rolling, athletic gait attracting the eyes of most of the females in the tavern.

He's off to find a place to sleep. The local hotel looks good. But, again, Thomas is out of folding money.

He walks back to his two best friends, who again are only too happy to help with directions to the local YMCA, where they say Thomas is sure to find a room and a bath.

"Just tell the guy at the counter you know us," says the guy who's been drinking at Thomas's right elbow.

The cop on the left slips out to the payphone to call ahead.

"I guarantee the police department will cover his bill," the officer says to the YMCA desk clerk. "Just give this guy coming over what he wants and send us the bill."

So, that's how Thomas will get the best night's sleep he'd had since leaving Alma's place. And tomorrow, he'll wear out some well-rested shoe leather on the sidewalks of Quincy. He's hoping to work just long enough to put some cash in his thin leather wallet before thumbing his next ride.

Meanwhile, FBI agents Ridell and Wilson, who've been riding and sleeping together for far too long, watch their prey from the uncomfortable confines of their Ford Coupe.

As soon as Thomas goes around the corner tomorrow, Ridell, who lost a coin toss challenge, will roust the YMCA desk clerk for the key to Thomas's room.

CHAPTER 25

This is hardly the first hotel room they've torn up. Wilson and Ridell have taken the time, per E.J.'s orders, to search every hotel room Thomas has stayed in wandering the Midwest.

He used an alias every time he stopped for a night or two, but there wasn't a desk clerk who couldn't identify a photo of Thomas. It wasn't just his dark, curly hair or bright smile hotel employees remembered.

"This guy just can't keep his mouth shut," Ridell says to Wilson after talking to the desk clerk at this YMCA in Quincy.

"You'd think even a dim bulb would be bright enough to know that he doesn't want anyone to remember him."

"But not our boy," says Ridell. He snorts and laughs, a habit that Wilson has had more than enough of.

"And he can't stay away from the ladies, can he?"

Wilson looks out the room's only window. The weather outside is as foul as the weather in Room 206.

Wilson sees Thomas walking on the side of the road. Looks like he's going into the factory district. Both Wilson and Thomas see a crack of lightning and hear a rumble of thunder. But only one gets soaked by a driving line of horizontal rain.

Thomas pulls his jacket up around his neck as Wilson laughs.

"Justice," he whispers.

"Oh, the ladies love him too." Ridell grunts as he bends down to grab the mattress on his side of the bed.

"Huh?"

"Give me a hand, will ya?"

Wilson puts both hands under the mattress on his side and

counts to three.

Ridell isn't paying attention to Wilson's countdown, so with the unity of a grammar school band, they flip the mattress into the air.

Ridell tosses his side first, higher and faster than Wilson does, so his partner is forced to catch the mattress before it crushes him.

Wilson struggles with the queen-sized mattress while he's cursing every ancestor perched in Ridell's family tree. But Wilson freezes when Ridell cheers.

"Look at this," says Ridell.

Wilson steps back and drops the mattress. He watches it hit the floor with a deep-throated thud. And he smiles to think how the people in Room 106 might have been surprised.

He looks up to see his buddy smiling from ear to ear.

It takes Wilson a moment to move his focus from Ridell's toothy grin, but he soon sees the reason for his partner's joy.

In Ridell's right hand, his partner is holding an old 32-caliber Colt revolver.

Wilson shouts, "Hey, will ya look at this?"

With a broad smile on his face, too, Wilson thinks about something else President Truman said in his Thanksgiving declaration back on November 22.

"…let us give thanks to Almighty Providence for these exceeding blessings."

"I guess that just about says it all," Wilson whispers.

Then, he claps his hands.

"So, who's going to call E.J. about this? Flip you for it."

CHAPTER 26

Thomas gets an envelope of cash after working one day at the first factory he walked into today. Now, strolling out of town, he's heading to the nearest highway. Once there, he'll start hitchhiking again.

Of course, the FBI is right behind him as the agents begin another long journey hoping Thomas will eventually lead them to Thora.

First, Thomas sticks out his thumb and hops a ride to Taylor, Missouri. From there, he'll make stops in Hannibal, Shelbina, Macon, Bevien, Brookfield, Chillicothe, and finally, St. Joseph, Missouri.

That's where a new squad of FBI agents take over the trail. They begin working in teams, just like their counterparts had, following Thomas.

From St. Joseph, Thomas keeps hitching rides and finally reaches Lexington, Nebraska. Then, agents from Nebraska begin following him and continue doing so until Thomas thumbs a ride to Denver.

The Nebraska FBI team radios their colleagues in Denver, and agents in that city take over the case. But they also relay the message to a couple of worn-out agents whose faces need to be kissed by the blade of the sharpest razor available.

These two, Ridell and Wilson, almost cheer when they see Thomas standing by the side of a road near Denver, carrying a scarred suitcase and a paper-wrapped package.

Ridell rolls down the driver's side window of the Ford Coupe and shouts, "Hey, pal, need a lift?"

It's not like Ridell and Wilson want Thomas with his days of road dust and sweat clinging to him like a second skin to be sitting between them.

"Would love to have a four-door with a backseat," Wilson whispers to Ridell.

But he knows if they don't give Thomas a ride, he will be camped out on this desolate road ignored by most travelers for who knows how long.

And so will Wilson and Ridell.

So, the two undercover agents pull over and offer Thomas a lift.

They seem friendly enough, Thomas thinks. Besides, he's so desperate, Thomas only hesitates a second or two before he hops in their car.

CHAPTER 27

Ridell and Wilson drop Thomas off at a bus station in Reno, Nevada.

Even though Thomas didn't tell them his plans for the immediate future, the agents are confident, or at least hopeful, they know where Mr. McMonigle is heading.

"He's gotta be going back to California, right?" Wilson says.

"You mean, San Mateo?" Ridell replies. "God, we can only hope."

Sure enough, Thomas catches the bus that takes him directly to the central bus terminal, where he boards a bus for Los Angeles.

And, he's got company.

Ridell and Wilson phoned ahead to their colleagues in Reno. Because of that call, two FBI undercover agents will be sitting in the same row as Thomas all the way to Los Angeles.

Ridell crosses his fingers while his partner's on the phone, asking E.J. if they should drive ahead of the bus to meet Thomas in L.A.

Ridell's holding out hope until he sees Wilson's shoulders slump as he hangs up the phone.

"No dice," Ridell whispers to himself.

Wilson launches himself back into the Ford after slamming the phone booth door shut hard enough to wobble the booth.

"The boss says we gotta follow this bus."

"So we're sucking down more diesel."

Ridell starts the car and moves forward quickly to catch up with Thomas's chariot to L.A.

"Anything else from E.J.?"

"He's going to have a team of LAPD black-and-whites and more of our agents waiting at the terminal. When McMonigle comes out of the bus, they grab him."

"They have enough to charge him?"

"Sounds like it." Wilson stares out the windshield.

"Or at least," Ridell says, "they've come up with enough to pull Mr. Thomas Henry McMonigle in for questioning and sweat him."

"And maybe then we can find Miss Thora Chamberlain."

CHAPTER 28

December 6, 1945

Everything's going as scheduled. A contingent of LAPD officers, county sheriff deputies, and of course the FBI is on hand to welcome Thomas home.

As the bus lumbers in, law enforcers remain at their posts, listening to the bus's brakes squeal and the door whoosh open. The bus driver hops down the steps and strides to the luggage door, which he pops open. The driver is a short bald man with the steering wheel's notches carved into his hands and the groves of the torn driver's seat engrained on his butt. Like he's done a million times before, the driver starts tossing valises and suitcases to the pavement.

Passengers, whose legs have not been stretched for hours, timidly creep down the bus's steps. It's early morning. Sun's just rising over the horizon. Nobody's moving quickly, at least not as rapidly as Wilson and Ridell would prefer.

Finally, the passengers are off. The bus driver helps them sort through luggage and even shakes hands with those he's made friends with during the journey.

At the same time, Ridell and Wilson share a cold shiver, along with a hard stare from their boss, E.J.

Where's Thomas?

There's no sign of McMonigle on the tarmac. It's not like it's a huge crowd standing beside the bus. Even though he's not the tallest guy in San Mateo, how could Thomas get lost amongst twenty or thirty people? Where are the agents who've been riding with him?

Ridell and Wilson, recovering from the cold shiver that ran up and down their spines, look at each other. Then out of the corners of their eyes, they see the bus driver bounding back up the steps into his vehicle.

Wilson and Ridell stare at each other for a moment before moving toward the bus. E.J. motions with his hand to direct the rest of the troops in the same direction.

Some of the FBI agents crouch without losing a step to look under other buses, to see if Thomas decided to hide out amongst the diesel and oil of a vehicle's underbody. The bus driver is moving back to the front of his big rig.

Wilson nudges Ridell's shoulder and points. The two undercover agents are coming out of the bus. So is the bus driver.

And someone's with the bus driver, or better put, the driver is carrying someone with him.

"Oh for Pete's sake," says Ridell

"It's McMonigle," E.J. and Wilson say.

Once he navigates Thomas's dead weight down the steps of the bus, the driver almost has to pour Thomas into Wilson's waiting arms.

More than groggy, Thomas is only semi-conscious. Eyelids fluttering like a hummingbird over a flower, drool dribbling out of the corner of his mouth. He's obviously trying to say something.

Ridell takes off his fedora and moves his ear close to Thomas's mouth. He's rewarded with the sound and rank stench of a belch.

Ridell almost punches Thomas in the mouth in response but catches E.J.'s stern look out of the corner of his eye. Ridell looks wistfully at his fist before shaking it out and putting his hand back in his pocket.

"Call an ambulance?" Wilson says.

"No time," says E.J. "Put the cuffs on him, throw him into the backseat of a squad car and get to the closest hospital as fast as you can. The last thing I want is this guy dying on us."

CHAPTER 29

December 8, 1945

E.J's pacing the hospital's hallway, head down, picking his way through the FBI agents and cops standing around with nothing better to do. Never a patient man, he is still usually calm. But it's been two days since they brought Thomas in, and there's still no word on when he'll be able to talk.

Finally, E.J. hears the soft shuffle of a nurse coming toward him. He looks up and sees she's got a smile on her face.

With a wink and a beckoning finger, she motions him to follow her.

"The doctor will see you now," she says. Of course the nurse is stating the obvious, but she also wants to make sure E.J. understands the intent of her somewhat forward behavior.

E.J.'s lips twitch under his thin mustache, and he smiles. No way will he follow her. E.J. moves quickly so that he is soon walking beside the young woman.

Inside an office, E.J. finds himself across from a doctor young enough to be his son. Yet, he waits respectfully for the medical man to speak first.

"It was sleeping pills," the doctor says, "an overdose."

"Damn. Suicide?"

"Close. If that was Mr. McMonigle's intent, he nearly pulled it off."

The young resident is enjoying his day in the sun, lecturing an FBI agent. He leans back in his chair with his fingers laced behind his head. E.J. thinks that with a quick kick, he'd have this youngster flat on his back. But he keeps that to himself, opting to let the doctor have his day.

"We had to pump his stomach. If you hadn't rushed him here, there's no doubt Mr. McMonigle would have suffered severe internal damage, or he would have died."

E.J. sits back to contemplate for a moment what would have happened to the investigation if Thomas had been successful.

In a moment, though, it's back to work.

"He's okay to leave now?"

"Yes," says the doctor. "Mr. McMonigle seems rational, mentally clear, and he seems well-oriented in all spheres."

The doctor pauses for a moment to make sure E.J. understands. The FBI Agent in Charge, the agency's kidnapping expert, lets the doctor know with a hard stare that he does.

The doctor gets the message. He nervously clears his throat puts his hands on the desk.

"His physical findings and neurological findings are also normal."

"So he's good to go?"

"In a phrase, Agent, he's all yours."

CHAPTER 30

Five high school girls, all Campbell Union High School students, and close friends of Thora's are in San Francisco today. Their parents are with them, but this is hardly a family vacation for anyone, nor is it a school field trip.

They've all been taken, at government expense, to San Francisco to hopefully identify the man who abducted Thora.

A month ago, E.J. showed the girls photos of six men and they all picked the picture of Thomas, identifying him as the man who drove off with Thora in his car.

Today, they are not going to be looking at photos. The girls will have to look at a lineup of six men, and hopefully choose, Thomas, again.

One after another, the girls and their parents stand in a darkened room, looking through a thick window into another room, which is well-lighted. In that second room, six men stand in front of a wall marked in inches and feet to show how tall they are. And, each man holds a cardboard sign, bearing a number, one through six.

The men stand about the same height — five feet nine to five feet eleven inches tall. And the half-dozen men, in their early thirties, each have bushy to curly black hair atop their heads.

"It's a lineup," Elaine Scimeca whispers to her mother. The fifteen-year-old child is fascinated. It's like she's walked into a movie. Elaine half expects Humphrey Bogart or Spencer Tracy to come into the room with her.

She's the last of the teenage girls to stand in the lineup room. The others have all identified the same man. If Elaine points him out, too, E.J. will be a giant leap closer to closing this case.

"Just take your time, Elaine," says E.J. He's standing alongside the girl, speaking softly. He sees she's trembling. But he can't tell if it's fear or excitement that has her so jumpy.

"Those men standing before you, one of them may be the man who drove off with Thora. But maybe not."

E.J. glances at Elaine's mother, who puts both of her hands on the girl's shoulders in a show of maternal support.

"Remember," E.J. says for the benefit of Elaine's mother as much as the child. "You can see them, but they cannot see you, and if you pick one, he will never know you identified him."

"Not unless or until she testifies in court," says Elaine's mother.

E.J. takes a breath and fixes his eyes on the woman standing behind Elaine. "That is correct, ma'am. And you and your daughter have to be prepared for that."

More than a moment's silence passes as everyone in the room appreciates the importance of the situation.

"Okay," says Elaine. "I'm ready."

She's holding her hands tight together under her chin. The excitement of actually being a part of a police lineup is fading. Now, even though she's not yet old enough to drive, Elaine feels the responsibility weighing upon her.

It's one of those moments when a child takes a step toward adulthood. Elaine's mother feels that, too, as her little girl moves away from her. Her mother's hands fall from her shoulders, Elaine looks at E.J. with determined eyes.

"He's here," Elaine says.

E.J. smiles. "Which one? Can you tell me the number he's holding in front of his chest?"

"Yes, sir, it's number five."

Her mother gasps. Does Elaine understand she's just identified a man who quite possibly kidnapped Thora Chamberlain and maybe even killed her? Will Elaine, her father, and I be ready to face this man in open court, her mother wonders.

"You are sure. The man who drove off with Thora, November 2nd, is here today, and he is holding a placard with the number five written on it," says E.J.

"Absolutely."

E.J. smiles. Five out of five. Batting 1.000. He's got the right man. Thomas Henry McMonigle.

Elaine breaks eye contact with E.J. She looks at the wooden-planked floor beneath her feet.

"I will never forget that man's face," says Elaine. She takes a breath so sharp it almost hurts.

"I told Thora not to go with him. I knew something was wrong, right away."

Elaine looks back at her mother.

"But she didn't listen. She never listens." Elaine looks at the floor, and at that moment, she knows she will never see her best friend again.

CHAPTER 31

December 12, 1945

Three long days of interrogation, and it doesn't look like McMonigle is going to crack. That's the sad assessment E.J. had to deliver to J. Edgar in Washington last night, and he could tell the boss was displeased.

Neither man was giving up hope that Thora was out there, somewhere alive. McMonigle, although suspected of sexually assaulting a girl about Thora's age, had no natural history of violence. At least not deadly violence.

Agents who spoke to Thomas's co-workers and wife came away without a single shred of evidence that the girl was dead. And through three days of intense grilling, Thomas had not come close to a confession.

So today, E.J. and his agents turn up the heat.

"It's a simple question, McMonigle. Thora Chamberlain. Where is she?" E.J. stands inches from the suspect, whose hands are cuffed behind him, holding him to the seat of a wooden chair.

Thomas uses his dark eyes to focus on whichever agent he's talking to. So, it seems that man is the only person in the room besides himself. Now, those eyes, still shining, are outlined by rivers of sweat that are just now coming from his thick black hair.

But, he's grinning.

E.J.'s fellow agents, including Wilson and Ridell, who are as sick of Thomas as any two humans could be, stand on either side of the suspect.

Thomas smiles as he looks from one to another, even trying to look over his shoulders to see if anyone is behind him.

However, even though he's smiling, Thomas seems out of it. Just like he was while being rushed to a hospital.

Does he even know where he is? E.J. wonders.

As the FBI's first and only kidnapping expert, E.J. has seen more than his share of men who abducted people for profit. Those cases were easy to understand.

A gangster needs quick cash, so he cases a wealthy family's home and life and finds a family member who is easy to grab. The kidnapper, in those cases, is also looking for a family with ready cash — liquid, as they say on Wall Street. And, above all else, he wants a family who will cave, come up with the greenbacks in small denominations, of course, and do the deal.

True, there were some cases of guys who were just bonkers, the ones where the motive was hard to figure out besides the fact that the guy was just a sicko. But in those cases, the suspects quickly started jabbering and had no interest in a murder rap.

But this time, this suspect, this Thomas McMonigle, lit up like he was on stage, laughing and smiling through every minute of his interrogation.

"Thora Chamberlain. You remember her, don't you?" E.J. pushes a black-and-white photo of the girl into Thomas's face.

Thomas perspires and begins breathing faster, quickly, like's he's running a race. But, still, he's smiling.

From his left, Ridell says, "you recognize that picture, don't you? And, guess what? We showed your photo to the girls Thora was with, her friends."

"Each one of them," says Wilson, his fist close enough to Thomas to make the suspect flinch, "identified you. Every one of those girls says you were behind the wheel of the car that Thora got into."

A bright desk lamp is shining on Thomas's face. Edwards and Harris come out from behind the light, approaching Thomas from either side.

"You drove away with Thora," says Edwards.

From the other side, Harris grabs Thomas's chin and roughly turns McMonigle's face to the left. E.J. passes Harris Thora's photo.

"Where is she?" Harris demands.

Thomas recoils from Harris's grip on his chin like he's been burned by a branding iron. The smile is gone. Even the curl in his hair seems to have gone limp.

E.J. pulls back from Thomas. His stomach tightens because he senses what's coming next. He's been in the presence of evil before and sees it in Thomas's face.

This guy has the look of the devil, E.J. thinks.

However, with a blink, Thomas's smile is back as he glances from one agent to another. Yet there is a different glint in his eyes. Thomas isn't enjoying this anymore. The limelight no longer holds the sick attraction it once had.

And E.J. knows the following words will be the two that he doesn't want to hear.

Thomas takes a deep breath, smiles, and says, "She's dead."

CHAPTER 32

The agents, all besides E.J., are shocked. With new lines of disbelief etched on their young faces, Wilson, Edwards, Harris, and Ridell back away into the shadows left by the desk lamp.

E.J. moves closer. He walks behind Thomas and unlocks the handcuffs before pulling a wooden chair up and sitting down.

Thomas's arms are numb. He's having trouble moving them into a position where he can get the blood flowing again.

E.J. stares into his eyes, giving Thomas time to get a bit more comfortable. As he focuses on the windows to Thomas's soul, he sees McMonigle's attention is wandering.

E.J. holds his hand close to Thomas's face and snaps his fingers loud enough to make McMonigle jump.

"You killed Thora Chamberlain," says E.J. It isn't a question; it's a statement. E.J. has been around more than one block with wackos like Thomas. Sick, weird, self-absorbed, vain, boastful, and living a fantasy life; all of those apply to Thomas, E.J. believes.

Yet, he's not ready to believe Thomas McMonigle is a killer. Or maybe he just doesn't want to believe Thora's dead.

Thomas looks at E.J. with a slight smile on his face and whispers, "yes, I think I killed her."

"How?"

Thomas licks his lips. E.J. reaches back for a glass of water that's been sitting on top of the desk all day. He hands it to Thomas. Not the freshest water, but killers can't be choosers.

Thomas gratefully drinks every drop.

He licks his lips again.

"I took her to Santa Cruze on Highway 17," Thomas says, "and got off on Highway 1."

"Close to the San Mateo County line?"

"Yeah."

"Why?"

"Well, the girl wasn't cooperating." Thomas looks into E.J.'s eyes. "It didn't have to go this way, but she just wouldn't shut up."

E.J. sighs. "So, Thomas, what did you do?"

"I just wanted to scare her, to get her to shut up. So, I reached into my glove box and got my gun."

"What kind of gun?"

Thomas shakes his head like he's been slapped. How dare E.J. interrupt his story.

"A Colt, a 32," says Thomas.

Thomas looks past E.J. and sees Ridell and Wilson looking at each other with raised eyebrows. Sounds like the gun they found in that YMCA in Quincy, they think, as Thomas reads their thoughts. He didn't know they had the gun, but now he does.

E.J. follows Thomas's eyes to the agents behind him and motions for Wilson and Ridell to back off. When he returns his attention to Thomas, E.J. sees McMonigle's eyes have clouded over. He's losing focus.

Thomas is groggy again, just like when he got off the bus.

"If I shot her, that is where it took place," he says.

The agents look at each other. That's hardly a firm statement of guilt.

E.J.'s worried about keeping Thomas awake or even conscious. The last thing he needs is for McMonigle to wind up in the hospital again.

Instead of snapping his fingers, E.J. gets up out of his chair and goes down on one knee in front of Thomas.

E.J. puts his hand on Thomas's knee, shocking the younger men standing behind him.

Suppose Thomas's murder confession is genuine and not some kind of fantasy or diversionary tactic. In that case, the most important thing now is finding the body. Taking this to trial without a corpse would be a prosecutor's worst nightmare.

And if it's not a homicide but still a kidnapping case, finding Thora is even more paramount.

So, the good-cop, bad-cop routine is history. No more shouting, yelling or threatening. It's time for a conversation.

"Is that where you left, Thora? Where you shot her?"

Thomas is silent for a moment. He's eye-to-eye with E.J.

"I didn't want to shoot her. That was never what I wanted to do."

"I know Thomas, we all know that, and we understand. What we need to know, what you must tell us, is where is Thora now?"

Thomas nods. He understands.

"I kept driving with her in the car. I drove north on Highway 1 to Devil's Slide. That's where I pulled over," he says. "I got her body out of the car and rolled it off a cliff into the water."

Oh, sweet Jesus, no, E.J. thinks. He stands and puts a hand on Thomas's shoulder.

Devil's Slide is a rugged ridge of rock, a promontory, on the San Mateo coast between Pacifica and Montara. It gets its name from massive landslides that plunge from the sharp, unforgiving, rocky edges of the cliff hundreds of feet in the air into the swirling water below.

If Thomas is telling the truth, the undertow and swell of the water are such that Thora's body was ripped to pieces only a few days after she was murdered. Maybe even a few hours.

E.J. moves away from Thomas as guards help him stand before walking him down the hall to a holding cell.

"Hey, wait!" E.J. marches down the hall after the guards and Thomas. He moves in front of the guy who just said he killed a fourteen-year-old girl, maybe by accident.

"You killed her in the car?"

Thomas looks at his feet.

"Up here! Look me in the eye, Thomas."

Once McMonigle complies, E.J. continues.

"You shot Thora Chamberlain to death in your Plymouth?"

Thomas nods his head.

"Could the bullet that killed her still be in the car, or do you think it was in her head when you tossed Thora off Devil's Slide?"

Thomas shakes his head. "No, not in her and not in the car. The bullet. I found it."

E.J.'s beyond red in the face. He's about to blow a gasket, and what comes out will rain down on Mr. McMonigle.

"Thomas. Look at me. Where is that bullet now?"

No reply. Stone-cold silence.

"Thomas," E.J. whispers. He glances back at his team of agents. "Thomas, my men, are losing patience, and so am I. Where is the bullet that killed Thora Chamberlain?"

Thomas sighs. His wise-ass grin melted off his face a few sentences ago. Now, he knows there's very little in his future except maybe a rendezvous with California's gas chamber.

"I dug it out of the wood doorpost between the front and rear seats on the passenger's side."

"And?"

"And, what?"

"And, Thomas, what did you do next?"

"And, I took the bullet home."

"Of course, he did," mutters Harris to his fellow agents.

"What did you do then, Thomas?" E.J. is inches from Thomas's face and seconds away from unleashing Ridell's fist.

"And, I took it home."

"You said."

"Then, I buried the slug in the backyard, under a tree, so nobody would ever find it."

CHAPTER 33

Thora's dead? The agents behind E.J. freeze in shocked disbelief. Everything they've done to date has been a waste.

Instead of rescuing an abducted child, the best they can hope for is recovering the body of a dead teenager.

E.J. stands slowly. He wears a smile that looks like it was chiseled in by Gutzon Borglum, the creator of Mount Rushmore.

Unfortunately, Gutzon didn't live long enough to see the colossal sculpture completed. He died a few months shy of the final drilling, about four years ago.

E.J., on the other hand, plans to be around to see his team recover Thora's body, along with any and all evidence of her murder. But even if doctors put him in on those iron lungs that have been around for about twenty years, E.J. makes a promise to himself.

And, he makes sure Thomas knows it.

"I will be here to see you die."

As Thomas is marched down the hallway, E.J. turns to his team, confronting the dejection of men who feel they have failed Thora and her family.

"Men, this is not the best news we could have hoped for, but at least it gives us a direction," says E.J. "If McMonigle did, in fact, kill Thora Chamberlain; we must recover her body."

The other agents, professionals to a man, nod their agreement.

"The prosecutors will need that for the trial, and more importantly, Thora's family needs to know. Her parents can't be left wondering if their little girl is dead or alive to the end of their days.

"Now, let's get to work."

With Thomas safely locked away in the San Mateo county jail, E.J decides to divide his team up into two units.

Back in their office, E.J. stands in front of his squad.

"Wilson, Ridell, and Harris; you go to McMonigle's home in San Mateo. Dig up the backyard and find the bullet he says he buried."

The trio nods their acquiescence, and their boss turns his attention to the other three agents.

"Edwards, Schultz, and McLaughlin; you're going with me to the Devil's Slide," E.J. says. "We are going to find Thora Chamberlain."

CHAPTER 34

December 16, 1945

Even in December, it's hot, sweaty work, digging up the backyard of the McMonigle home in San Mateo. Agents Wilson, Ridell, and Harris take turns using a shovel and spade to dig up earth around a tree. The third is on his hands and knees with a trowel, painstakingly looking for a .32-caliber slug.

The men shucked their coats into the backseat of their Ford soon after arriving at the McMonigle's and notifying Thomas's wife of their warrant to search the backyard.

Wilson, Harris, and Ridell ditched their ties, too, after only an hour with the spade, shovel, and trowel. The three kept their fedoras in place. Fashion counts for something, as does J. Edgar's dress code.

Wilson and Ridell lean on a shovel and spade, respectively, watching Harris use a trowel to shift through a pile of dirt.

"This could take the rest of the day," says Wilson.

Ridell agrees. "Hey, take it easy. Slow down," he urges Harris. "This slug is all smashed up."

"The bullet went through the girl and then lodged in the wood frame of the car's doorpost."

"It's not even going to look like much anymore."

"You think I'm a dope," says Harris. On his knees, realizing there's no way even the best dry cleaner in town is going to save these trousers, Harris carefully scoops through the ground.

He looks up at his partners.

"Don't you think you two ought to be on your hands and

knees helping me?"

Ridell and Wilson grudgingly comply. Both squat down, hoping to spare their pants from the fate suffered by Harris's trousers.

Since Harris has the only trowel, Wilson sticks his fingers into the dirt clods before him and mashes the earth like a child making a mud pie.

"Hey," he yells, 'I've got something."

CHAPTER 35

Ruining a pair of trousers is the last thing on the minds of agents Edwards, Schultz, McLaughlin, and Connelley.

While their fellow FBI agents are digging up the McMonigle's San Mateo yard, each of the G-men quartet slowly makes their way down the side of Devil's Slide.

A sixty-foot length of rope around each man's waist is the only thing keeping them from falling more than 300-feet to their deaths in the swirling water and jagged rocks below.

With the other end of the ropes lashed to their Ford sedan's front bumper, the agents pick their way through rocks and boulders while going down the steep, sheer Slide.

Nobody's saying a word, fearing any distraction could cause them or another agent to slip, slide and fall to certain death.

However, their faces showed a steely determination. The agents wondered during the drive here if they might find Thora's body.

None of the agents wanted to imagine what a fall from the cliff into that maelstrom could do to a human body.

But, nobody looking down into the churning waters swirling around craggy, rough, uneven boulders holds out any hope for Thora now.

So, instead of looking for Thora, the agents search for any evidence, clothing, school books, anything that helps prove Thomas's story.

The only hope they have of closing this case is to find evidence that McMonigle and Thora were here, and of course, that Thora is dead.

So, they refuse to concede defeat.

At the same time, the agents know that the slightest misstep could result in their deaths.

Finally, after hours of searching, their efforts bear fruit.

"I've got something." McLaughlin holds up two pairs of red and blue socks that he found stuck in the rocks about two-thirds of the way down the cliff.

E.J., hanging as perilously close to death as his three agents, takes a deep breath.

Four socks aren't much, but how else would they have wound up here unless Thora's body was tossed off the cliff above and bounced off these rocks into the water below.

But still, E.J. can't be sure until Thora's parents identify the articles of clothing.

Looking down again, E.J. thinks he'd almost prefer being smashed to death in the swirling waters below rather than show these two sets of socks to one set of grieving parents.

But before he goes knocking on the Chamberlain's door, E.J. knows that if his men found two sets of socks on the cliffs, the body of the girl who wore them might be below in the water.

This is one search his men are not capable of.

"Okay, that's it," E.J. shouts. "Let's get out of here. And damn it, be careful pulling yourselves up."

"What's next boss," asks one of the agents.

Says E.J., "It's time to call the U.S. Navy."

CHAPTER 36

As if he needed one more thing on his plate, the three concrete and steel pillboxes on Devil's Slide remind E.J. of just how recent the Second World War was and how close the world came to Hitler's domination.

His men, all combat veterans of the conflict who learned to relax whenever they had the opportunity, stand around smoking Lucky's, recovering from their trek down the side of this jagged, rocky slope.

E.J.'s also catching his breath. But, like any good C.O., he knows there's a time when the officers need to give the enlisted their space. So, instead of smoking with his team, E.J. concentrates on the history of this God-forsaken place.

He checks out three other military structures — two bunkers made of concrete and dirt and a steel observation tower.

All are remnants of military life before the invention of radar, keeping an eye out for planes with a rising sun insignia leading a Japanese invasion.

"Thank God, they never got closer than Hawaii," mutters E.J., though he knows there were reports of enemy subs off the California coastline.

No matter how many years pass, E.J. hopes the U.S. never forgets how tenuous is its grip on democracy and freedom.

He sighs, shakes off his stroll down memory lane, and walks over to the new search crew that showed up when E.J. called in a favor to an old military buddy.

He picks his way carefully through the hardscrabble terrain to the edge of the cliffs.

Other than what the military left behind, someone who's not native to the region would be excused for thinking they'd somehow been transported to a strange, alien land.

Devil's Slide's steep, rocky slopes aren't friendly to much vegetation except riparian willow scrub, coastal grassland, and brushland.

The vegetation that sticks out over the water and the unweathered orange rocks are evidence of the landslides that give Devil's Slide its name.

If there was ever a place on Earth that could be a portal to Hell, this would be it, E.J. thinks.

While E.J. talks to their team leader, U.S. Navy divers, all with World War II Pacific Theater combat experience, are in the water below Devil's Slide. The scuba team's been in the water for a couple of hours. To a man, the divers are battered, bruised, and exhausted.

One of the team is worse off than the rest.

"What's with him?" E.J. points at a guy in a scuba suit sitting on the back of an ambulance. A red stream of blood flows from the top of the man's head, down his cheek to his neck.

Opposite E.J., a navy man who's obviously the team leader isn't about to be bull-rushed by a suit with an FBI badge no matter how well the agent knows his commanding officer.

"And you are?"

E.J. downshifts his personality back into government gear and produces his FBI credentials. After a quick introduction and handshake, he and the navy captain are on speaking terms.

"Damn bad down there," says the captain. "My men haven't seen water like this since, well, maybe never."

"That guy there has been knocked out cold, unconscious three times by the swirling water."

E.J. rubs his pencil-thin mustache.

"Any sign of the girl," he asks.

The navy captain gives him a grim smile.

"Not a sign and I'm not sure you're ever going to find her body.

Not if it was thrown off this cliff."

"Not a chance?"

"Nope. These waters are so rough we couldn't use a diving bell. It would have been smashed to pieces on the jagged rocks underwater. My men are fighting twenty-foot swells."

E.J. sees four large cables hanging into the water.

"Those are 350-foot cables," explains the navy team leader. "We're lowering our men down on those. Some of the guys have even gone down without scuba gear, hoping they could fight the currents better."

He pauses to light a fresh Camel.

"But no luck."

The navy captain flips his lighter closed.

"I'm willing to exhaust every available means," he says. "But if your girl's body was tossed off this cliff into that water, she'd be torn to pieces in two or three days."

"Great. Thanks."

E.J. sighs.

"I'll spare the parents your analysis. They'll have enough to deal with for the rest of their lives without knowing a school of hungry sharks ate their child after she was smashed and ripped to shreds."

"But, you know what, boss?" One of the agents leans into the conversation. "It makes me want to nail this son of a bitch McMonigle even more."

CHAPTER 37

E.J. told Ridell to "step on it" after his team piled into their Ford.

However, E.J. hesitates as he and his men step up to the porch of Thora Chamberlain's home. His knuckles are raised to knock on the front door, but E.J. freezes for a moment.

Then, he knocks, and Thora's father, Frank, quickly throws open the front door. His wife, Lois, is standing behind him with her arms around Thora's two younger sisters. Eight-year-old Sherrill and her five-year-old sister Carol have tears in their eyes. Lois looks over her husband's shoulder at E.J.

The FBI's kidnapping expert has seen more than enough women wearing the same sad yet hopeful expression as is on Lois's face.

Could there be hope that her little girl will be brought home alive? Is Thora, in fact, alive and well, and sitting in the Ford?

Lois wears the look of a woman fearing the worst yet, praying for the best.

Frank, on the other hand, is one of San Jose's leading businessmen — a contractor — who's accustomed to receiving bad news. Yet, despite his sturdy, square jaw, it's easy to see he's also nervous.

E.J. smiles at Mrs. Chamberlain but focuses most of his attention on the head of the household.

Frank Chamberlain adjusts his wire-rimmed glasses and steps aside, wordlessly inviting E.J. into his home.

While the rest of the team waits on the porch, E.J. doffs his fedora and recently blocked hat in hand, enters the Chamberlain house.

Never one to be the least bit self-conscious, E.J. is a bit more humble than usual. He's used to coming with good news.

"Your daughter has been found alive and well, and we have arrested her abductors," is what E.J. says typically. Because, usually, he solves kidnappings, not murders.

This time though, it's not an abduction case. It's looking more and more like a homicide. And it's a long way from being solved.

On top of that, E.J. knows the sand and dirt of Devil's Slide hides in the cuffs of his trousers.

His face is also streaked with sweat and dirt, despite E.J.'s failed attempt to clean up in a service station restroom.

But, E.J. knows he not only has trained FBI agents waiting outside, every minute that goes by makes this case colder and more unsolvable.

He gets to the purpose of the visit. E.J. pulls the two pairs of socks discovered on Devil's Slide out of his pocket.

Lois gasps and walks from the living room to a hallway. She stops and looks back over her shoulder at E.J.

Wordlessly, he follows.

Lois leads him to a bedroom, obviously the room where Thora laid her head nightly, dreaming the fantasies, wishes, and hopes of all teenage girls.

Books and papers are still scattered on a small desk, a light film of dust is evidence on the window sill, and it appears Thora neglected to make her bed before leaving for school a month ago.

Lois runs her fingers through her short, brunette hair. Like her husband, she adjusts her glasses. She hasn't touched this room since Thora vanished, and although he has no children, E.J. feels like he understands.

Still, without saying a word to him, Lois strides across the room to a wooden dresser. She grasps the handles of the top drawer and slides it open.

E.J. doesn't move. He might not even be breathing while he waits for his next set of wordless instructions.

Lois leaves the drawer open and steps back. She nods in E.J.'s direction, and he moves to the dresser.

Stopping in front of it, he nods briskly to Lois and looks into the drawer.

No surprise. It's filled with red and blue bobby socks that look just like the four he's been carrying in his pocket since Devil's Slide.

CHAPTER 38

There's no time to waste. E.J shakes the hands of Thora's loving, grieving parents and moves to leave the home that's lighter by one.

A last look back breaks E.J.'s heart.

It's not that E.J.'s resolve to solve this case and bring Thomas Henry McMonigle to justice could be any more firm. But if his spine needed strengthening, the sight of two people softly weeping on each other's shoulders turns his backbone into titanium.

He runs down the steps to the Ford.

"Let's go, now. Schultz, you drive." E.J. tosses him the keys.

Schultz raises his eyebrows to ask the answer to the most apparent one-word question anyone who gets behind the wheel of a 1942 Ford would ask.

E.J. doesn't even look in Schultz's direction.

"We are going to the construction yard where McMonigle worked."

Schultz gets behind the wheel, drops it into first gear, and fires up the engine.

"Talking to the workers?"

"Nope. Digging for evidence. Two other agents are going to join us, Fred Elledge and Michael Farrin."

With one hand on the steering wheel, Schultz looks into the rearview and sees the other agents pushing their way into the back seat.

"Digging?"

"Yes. Remember what you and McLaughlin told me about

McMonigle working on filling in a ditch the last day he was at that construction yard in Burlingame?"

"Sure. His buddies said they'd never seen him work so hard or so fast."

"Right. And why do you think that was?"

Schultz pushes down on the accelerator with his right foot while letting the clutch out with his left. He shrugs his shoulders, then turns with a smile toward E.J.

"Because McMonigle had something to bury, maybe lots of stuff to bury, right boss?"

"Exactly what I'm thinking, and now we are going to go dig it all up."

CHAPTER 39

E.J. and his team stare at Thomas, who sits across from them in the San Mateo county jail's only conference room big enough to host this meeting.

Agents Ridell and McLaughlin stand by a blackboard on the wall facing Thomas. Both are still using their fingers to dig dirt out of their ears, a job that may never end after the day and night E.J. put them through.

Elledge and Farrin are beside them, the newest members of the team.

The agents spent much of last night digging up Thomas's last day of work in the construction yard. What they found is now set up on a long wooden table that separates the agents from Thomas.

"What do you think of all of this, Thomas?" E.J. stands behind the table. He stares at the man who killed a little girl. E.J. fixes Thomas with the glare that's broken many a gangster.

Thomas gulps and looks at Ridell, who always seems to have a fist ready for his face, and then back down at the table.

It's all here, Thomas thinks. He slowly nods his head.

Along with a pair of slate-gray trousers, which Elledge discovered, he sees Thora's brown shoes, her school books, a zipper binder, and the cowbell she planned to ring in celebration at the Nov. 2 football game.

The agents cleaned up the evidence the best they could, but it's evident that it all came from under the ground.

But that's not all. Thomas also sees the agents discovered the footlocker, about four feet long, plainly marked as belonging to a

U.S. military serviceman.

And they dug up a .32-caliber gun and pieces of bloody upholstery.

E.J. looks over the evidence table too. He slowly walks the length of the table.

It all makes sense. Each piece and part has its place in the puzzle of what happened to Thora Chamberlain and who is responsible.

Except for one thing, E.J. takes a fountain pen from the inside pocket of his suit coat and uses it to lift up a piece of the upholstery.

"What is this?"

Thomas takes a deep breath. E.J. sees his face is bruised, perhaps from an encounter with a jail guard, but more probably a dust-up with his fellow prisoners.

E.J. also sees the face of a man who's ready to talk. It's the countenance of a guy who's fallen into a deeper pile of manure than he's ever tried to dig himself out of before.

"That's from my Plymouth."

"Your car?"

"Yeah, I mean 'yes, sir,' it's the upholstery from the front seat, passenger side."

E.J. sighs and sets the upholstery back down on the table. Before he puts the fountain pen back in his pocket, he wipes it off with a handkerchief. He tosses the monogrammed linen aside.

"Why would you cut out and then bury a piece of upholstery from your car?"

Thomas looks down at the table then back up at E.J.

"Had to bury it cuz so much blood came gushing out of the girl's mouth after I shot her."

E.J. puts a hand back to stop Ridell from charging over the table and killing Thomas on the spot.

"I cut and ripped the upholstery out of the car," Thomas says. He flashes just a hint of a smile Ridell's way.

"There was so much blood, I knew I'd never get the upholstery clean again."

CHAPTER 40

E.J. would feel better if Thomas were cold, distant, and unfeeling about the blood gushing from Thora's mouth. Instead, this killer, who pretty much confessed today, is flippant.

What kind of a monster are we dealing with? The agents behind E.J. look at each other in a combination of amazement and disgust.

Shaking his head in revulsion, E.J. moves to another piece of evidence; a pair of slate-gray trousers.

"Yours?

Thomas looks at E.J. like he's just landed from the Moon or Mars.

E.J. plants both hands on the table. He picks up the trousers and holds them inches from Thomas's eyes.

"These trousers, are they yours?"

Thomas backs away and looks around the trousers at E.J.

"Not actually. No. Now that I think about it, those pants are not mine."

E.J.'s face flushes red, not with embarrassment but anger.

"Are these the trousers you were wearing on November 2nd when Thora Chamberlain was in your car?"

"Well, yes, if you put it that way." Thomas nods.

"We found these trousers buried with the rest of this evidence. Why did you bury them?"

Thomas takes a deep breath, glances at the floor, then the agents behind E.J. before answering the question with a smirk.

"Had to bury them." He shrugs. "Too much blood. I tried to wash it out, got most of it, but I was afraid there was still some blood in the seams of the pants or maybe the pockets."

E.J. stands straight and waits for the rest.

"So," Thomas says, "I buried the trousers with the rest."

Again he shrugs and smirks as he look from one agent to another.

"What else was I going to do?"

Finally, the last and most important piece of evidence between E.J. and Thomas — a .32 caliber pistol.

E.J. uses his fountain pen to push the gun toward Thomas. Neither man speaks. Thomas and E.J. are focused on the gun. Together they raise their eyes and look at each other.

"Well," says E.J. "Is this the weapon that you used to kill Thora Chamberlain?"

Thomas doesn't lose his smirk. But this is more than an adult trying to act like an adolescent. Thomas refuses to break eye contact with E.J.

"I know something happened in the car," Thomas whispers.

"If I did kill her, and I am not saying I did, but if I did, then yes, it might be the gun that I used, if I used a gun."

CHAPTER 41

Today, as they assemble for their morning meeting, E.J. is sitting at the table in the front of the room. The agents sit in the wooden chairs, each with a small desk attached, furniture that belonged in a schoolroom.

A week ago, Ridell asked what was on everyone's mind.

E.J. hadn't waited for the coldness of Thomas's reply to the question about whether he used the .32 caliber gun found in his backyard to kill Thora to sink in. Instead, he turned to Wilson, nodded, and Wilson walked to the conference room's door.

He motioned for the county deputies in the hallway. There was nothing else to do but send Thomas back to his cell.

Thomas left, with a burly county deputy on each side, holding his shackled arms.

Once the room was clear, Ridell pointed to the 500-pound elephant in the room.

"And what else are we going to do, boss?"

"Simple. We write this up and go to the prosecutor."

Now, it was McLaughlin's turn to speak his mind.

"We have everything we need, boss?"

E.J. nodded. Carefully, he placed all the evidence back into cardboard boxes.

"Yes, we have it all."

Then E.J. stopped packing up the evidence.

"Except," he said.

"Yeah," said Schultz. "Except one thing. Thora Chamberlain."

At that point, before going to the prosecutor, the agents followed their agency's procedure. They sent the boxed-up evidence against Thomas to the FBI laboratory in Washington D.C.

The pace of the investigation slowed over the past fourteen days. But the agents haven't been sitting on their thumbs. Instead, they've been out in the field interviewing everyone they could find who had any connection to Thomas, past or present.

Today, the agents wait. E.J. is reading a packet of information, slowly turning one page after another. No one wants to risk raising his ire, so nobody says a word. Instead, they look at each other, sigh, chew gum, smoke cigarettes, and twiddle their thumbs.

As the agents have learned the past couple of months, waiting is a significant part of the game when you're on E.J.'s team.

Finally, he senses his team is about ready to bust wide open. E.J. sets down the packet, looks at his men, and the pencil-thin mustache about his upper lip twitches.

He smiles. But it's not a grin of joy; instead, it's a steely look of determination.

"The laboratory technicians confirm all of our suspicions," says E.J.

The men in front of him stifle a cheer as he raises a hand.

E.J. puts his hand down and uses it to lift the packet written by their brother agents wearing white coats in the FBI lab.

"This confirms that there is human blood on the auto upholstery."

"Yes," says Riddle. Back slapping breaks out among the agents.

Using the power of silence worthy of the loud bang of any judge's gavel, E.J. waits for the agents to return to adulthood.

"The technicians are also confident the bullet discovered in the ground outside McMonigle's house did come from the .32-caliber Colt that we found buried in the ditch near his workplace."

Wilson pumps his fist in the air.

"So, assuming McMonigle was telling the truth," E.J. says, "we have the bullet the gun that killed Thora Chamberlain. And, most importantly, we have the man, I believe, who pulled the trigger."

The FBI agents sit back in their chairs. Although they were initially joyful, the men understand collecting evidence and even filing a murder charge is only part of the mission.

Again, Ridell speaks for the room.

"Boss, do we have enough to nail this son of a bitch?"

E.J. uses the thumb and forefinger of his right hand to stroke his mustache.

"Yes," he says. "We have it all."

And then, after a sigh, E.J. says, "we have it all, except for one thing."

"Yeah," says McLaughlin. "Thora Chamberlain."

CHAPTER 42

December 17, 1945

Leaders of the new United Nations Organization, this week, are dealing with the bitterness of European heads of state dissatisfied with the decision to place the new "Capital of the World," the headquarters of the "UNO" somewhere in the United States.

Ena McMonigle doesn't care. She's trying to figure out how her life could have gone down the crapper so quickly.

Ena didn't learn of Thomas's confession until reading about it in the San Mateo Times. Not only was she shocked, but Ena also couldn't believe Thomas could kill a teenage girl.

"It's horrible," the former Ena Izzard Bughi tells a neighbor and claims she never had any clue that her husband would do something like this.

"If it's all true, he must have been mad," Ena says.

Just two days before Thora disappeared, Ena gave birth to Thomas's child, and "he told me," Ena says, "'now I have something to live for.'"

She takes a breath with tears in her eyes.

"How could he have done this?"

Well, she convinces herself, Thomas did not do it. Given her husband's stellar work record, Ena refuses to believe that he could be a killer.

"Thomas worked as a guard with the Loomis armored car organization and for ADT Alarm," Ena stresses. "And he once caught a burglar."

"But didn't he leave you in the middle of the night," the neighbor asks.

"He told me he was going to visit his sick grandfather," says Ena. "And he constantly wrote and telephoned. Not once did he show he was in trouble."

Ena's first clue that something was wrong came when her friends and relatives called to say the FBI had been out to talk to them about Thomas.

And then, the FBI came knocking on Ena's door.

"They took everything out of the car, even the ceiling light. I told them all I knew. I have nothing to hide," she says.

"If this is true, he must be the victim of some mental quirk, which was never made known to his loved ones."

Before they were married, Thomas was always courteous, well-spoken, and a real gentleman, Ena claims.

But, later, after they became man and wife, Ena admits he changed.

It was only then Ena learned her husband had been in prison "and of his bitterness against the world."

She says Thomas told her, with "a great deal of bitterness,:" what it was like to be arrested and imprisoned when he was only seventeen years of age.

On top of that, Thomas found himself in solitary confinement for many hours during his time behind bars.

"Once he was released, each time he would get a new job, Thomas lived in fear his record would be learned. He brooded over it," Ena explains.

Yet, she refuses to not give her husband the benefit of the doubt.

"Whatever he's done, if it is true, I am sure it's a result of a bitter childhood."

Of course, Ena is hardly a mental health professional. Maybe she missed something.

According to every law enforcement man who's spent time with the accused killer, Thomas has a "persecution complex."

And, Dr. C.C. Gans, the San Mateo County health department

director, says he saw that mental health condition on full display when Thomas wasn't promoted to the job of captain of the county ambulance drivers a few months ago.

"McMonigle stormed into the health department offices and raised hell," says Dr. Gans. "McMonigle took the attitude that he was being persecuted."

CHAPTER 43

December 18, 1945

Everyone in San Jose and San Francisco will be able to read tomorrow that General George S. Patton's condition is improving. His neck was broken in an automobile accident eight days ago in Germany.

Doctors say there's been a gradual improvement of the warrior's motor functions, especially around his shoulders and upper chest.

Meanwhile, from Nuremberg, Germany will come news from the trial of the accused war criminals. Judges are heckling American prosecutors, saying they're overwhelmed by documents connected to "small fry" Nazis.

Cases against twenty-one of Hitler's top henchmen seem strong.

But journalists overseas will forecast the judges' irritation is casting doubt on whether American lawyers will be able to after lower-level Nazi groups.

That's all well and good. But everyone along California's shoreline today is talking today about a guy named Thomas Henry McMonigle and a young girl, a dead child, named Thora Chamberlain.

Thomas rides from San Quentin to the courthouse this morning alongside Sheriff William Emig and three deputy sheriffs. Following them in a second car are two more deputies packing shotguns and riot gear.

"We're just taking precautions," Sheriff Emig explains to a pack of reporters outside the courthouse. "The feeling is tense against McMonigle in San Jose."

Once Thomas is inside the courthouse, Santa Clara County grand jury speedily returns with indictments against Thomas on relatively mild kidnapping and child stealing charges. District Attorney Leonard Avilla decides not to ask for invocation of California's "Little Lindbergh" law. It would allow a jury to determine — assuming they vote to convict — whether Thomas should be sentenced to death or life in prison.

Avilla decides more severe charges like Little Lindbergh and murder will wait until Thora's body is recovered.

Thomas proclaims his innocence during the arraignment proceedings despite the grand jury's indictments and what the FBI says he told them.

He also announces his intention to ditch his public defender in favor of hiring his own counsel.

Outside the court building, Thomas runs into another squadron of reporters and continues to profess his innocence.

"They say I confessed, but I didn't," says Thomas standing tall, stretching to his total height of six feet and three inches, which puts him head and shoulders above many of the scribes scribbling with pencil and paper.

"I was unconscious when I arrived at the bus depot in San Francisco. When I came to, I was in the FBI's detention center at 111 Sutter Street."

"If you are innocent," says one of the reporters, "how and why did you lead the FBI to Devil's Slide where her bobby socks were found?"

Thomas doesn't hesitate. He replies, "I just took them to the spot where I had parked with the girl."

Thomas went on to admit he'd been drinking.

"I fell asleep and was awakened by a gunshot," says Thomas. "That's when I discovered the girl was gone."

CHAPTER 44

December 30, 1945

San Mateo and Santa Clara county officials settle their squabble over who would prosecute Thomas first, and in whose county jail he'd be housed awaiting trial.

Now, Santa Clara County Sheriff William Emig doesn't care if Thomas is innocent or guilty. But still, the sheriff can't stop himself from asking if he killed the girl.

After all, Sheriff Emig is the law in this county.

"You killed her, how? You shot Thora Chamberlain?"

"Shot who? Whattaya talking about? I didn't shoot anybody."

"Tell the truth, McMonigle. We know you shot the girl and threw her body off Devil's Slide into the ocean."

"I didn't dump anybody off a cliff."

"Thomas, come on. You already confessed to the FBI."

"I don't remember confessing to nobody."

"And you don't recall killing the girl?"

"Hey. Sheriff, if I done anything like that, I ought to pay for it. But I didn't."

Whether McMonigle is guilty or innocent, Emig learned a valuable lesson, a dozen years ago. And he is not going to let it happen again.

Back then, one of San Jose's favorite sons, Brooke Hart, had been kidnapped and murdered, allegedly by Thomas Thurmond and John M. Holmes.

The suspects were housed inside Santa Clara's county jail.

Did the people of San Jose demand justice? No, they wanted

blood.

A San Jose radio station, KQW, broadcast an announcement of plans for a lynching party. The station even gave its listeners the time and date of the bloody event.

Was Sheriff Emig concerned? Nope. He was confident in November 1933 that his jail was secure enough to withstand a citizen assault. Indeed, he assured the San Jose Lions Club that the facility was like a fortress.

Well, guess what? Here's the lesson Emig learned the hard way.

Thousands stormed the jail, shoving aside deputies and pulling Thurmond and Holmes outside.

Then, as KQW broadcast live from a downtown park, the two men were stripped naked, beaten bloody, and their arms broken when they resisted the mob.

A couple of sturdy ropes were tossed over two trees, nooses placed around the necks of Thurmond and Holmes, and the men were lynched.

The bodies hung for hours from the trees in this public park before being cut down.

So, if there is anyone in California who understands the potential of mob violence, it is Sheriff Emig. And he is not about to let that happen again.

That's why, as soon as Thomas is formally arrested, he is not taken to a cell in the county jail. Instead, after a brief stay in the Santa Clara monty jail he is shipped off to San Quentin State Prison to be housed on Death Row.

Today, Thomas will be out of prison, albeit briefly. He's getting a day in court, a preliminary hearing on the charges he faces in the kidnapping and presumed death of Thora Chamberlain.

More than aware of how enraged the Santa Clara County populace is over the case, Emig surrounds Thomas with a squadron of heavily armed guards as soon as McMonigle steps outside San Quentin.

All the way to the courthouse, Thomas is in an armored car, sitting with the armed guard, not to make sure he stays in custody, but to prevent the good citizens of Santa Clara County from killing him.

Ever the lover of the spotlight, Thomas, with the shackles around his body, hobbles to the car and into the county building with a jaunty smile on his face.

Flashbulbs explode outside. Inside, the atmosphere in the Santa Clara County courtroom crackles with tension.

This is a complicated case for Thomas's court-appointed defense attorneys, Stanford Smith and Bert Snyder, and the district attorney who'll prosecute the case, Stephen Wyckoff.

Here's why: As soon as Thomas was tossed into the hell hole that is San Quentin's Death Row, he starts changing the story of what happened between him and Thora.

First, Thomas claims he didn't shoot Thora. Instead, he choked her to death. Another time Thomas says he neither shot nor choked Thora; he stabbed her to death. And another time, he says he didn't toss Thora's body off a cliff; but buried her in a drainage ditch near the construction yard where he worked.

"This guy is so confused and telling so many different stories," Stephen Wyckoff says, "I'm worried about convincing a jury that this is actually a murder case."

Wyckoff tells E.J.'s team, "We need to find Thora's body."

The agents go back to Blain Construction Co., this time armed with a backhoe. They start digging up the drainage ditch at the construction yard.

But, it's all for naught.

"There's nobody buried here," the agents report back to E.J. and Wyckoff.

So, today, as Thomas's chains are removed, and he sits down behind the courtroom's defense table, Wyckoff knows he will have to make his case with the evidence that he has.

God knows there is plenty of evidence of, and witnesses to, the abduction, but there is no corpse. So there is no absolute proof that Thora is dead.

Wyckoff looks over his shoulder at the courtroom gallery, packed with reporters from all over California and even New York. The kidnapping and supposed murder of a teenage girl is front-page news from coast to coast.

And, believe it or not, Thomas has become something of a sex symbol.

Even though he's done time behind bars for rape and is accused of murder and kidnapping, thousands of women are mesmerized by this man.

So notebooks and pencils out, the reporters don't want to miss a word of what is coming.

In a few minutes, Wyckoff hears those reporters going wild as Thomas repudiates all of the confessions he's made the past few weeks.

Despite all the stories he told in days previous, Thomas says today that he did not kill Thora. Instead, Thomas says that they got lost while he and Thora were together, driving to Santa Cruz.

Oh, he admits being with the teenager, but Thomas claims he did nothing wrong. But precisely what happened to Thora, well, it's a mystery to him too.

"We got lost, and then I started drinking.

"Suddenly, I heard a shot," Thomas says, "and I turned around, and the girl was gone."

He shrugs. "That's all I can tell you."

Before the day is done, McMonigle enters two pleas: not guilty and not guilty by reason of insanity.

In a victory for the prosecution, the judge rules there is enough evidence to charge Thomas under the Federal Kidnapping Act, known in most quarters as the Lindbergh Law. And he decides the trial will commence next month.

With that, Thomas is re-shackled, the armed guards surround him again, and he's taken out to an armored car for a ride back to San Quentin.

The armed guards and their convoy will bring Thomas back to court for trial next month.

If he's convicted, Thomas will only leave his cell on Death Row following the trial, one more time, for the short walk to the gas chamber. If he's convicted, there will be no alternative but capital punishment.

CHAPTER 45

February 1, 1946

A jury is about to be seated — six women and five men — tasked with determining whether he kidnapped and killed Thora. They will decide whether he lives or dies.

It seems that Thomas wouldn't have anything else on his mind.

After all, Thomas knows his life is in the hands of a couple of public defenders, unless he represents himself, and he'll have to wait it out here in a cramped prison cell on San Quentin's Death Row.

But that is not what he's thinking about at the moment. Thomas's life just got turned upside down, again.

Everybody's got problems -- for instance, an Army lieutenant who's part of the U.S. occupation force in Germany. Today, Jack Burroughs's Oakland Tribune "This Is Your Town" column tells the story of this Sad Sack whose truck had a broken axle.

Like most of his G.I. buddies over there, the lieutenant doesn't speak much German. He relies on a book from a University of California extension course in German language and literature to survive in Berlin.

The lieutenant writes to his instructor, Franz Schneider, back home to complain that nothing in this book tells him how to say he needs to get the broken axle repaired.

Franz, an associate professor in German, tells Burroughs that he's not surprised his student has this problem.

"The truth is," says Professor Schneider, "that when we planned these courses, we had no idea they would be used by American occupation troops. Some of the material is likely to be on a little higher literary level than garage instructions."

So everybody has problems.

But today, Thomas Henry McMonigle thinks his problems are the worst in the world.

For, today, on his way back to a lonely, cold, Death Row prison cell, he is served divorce papers from his Ena.

Thomas's world is crushed. His eyes mist over as he reads a certified letter handed to him by Deputy Sheriff L.D. Kennedy.

Ena is suing for divorce, charging extreme cruelty, and asking for custody of their daughter, born just three months ago.

The blood and confidence drain from Thomas's face. His hands shake as he looks up at the smirking guard.

"Somebody must have put her up to doing this," Thomas says. "I cannot understand it because ours is not one of those here-today, gone-tomorrow marriages.

"I don't think she really means it."

Once he's back into his cell, looking forward to a weekend recess of his trial, Thomas collects himself and demands to see his lawyers.

Monday, the jury who will decide his fate should be seated. His court-appointed attorneys, Stanford Smith and Bert Snyder are ready to present their case — they thought.

But once they begin talking to Thomas, the plans of Smith and Snyder for a weekend of peace go out the window.

Thomas is holding the tear-stained divorce papers in his hand. His face is pale, his chin trembling before Thomas takes a deep breath.

"Listen. There's been a change," Thomas says to the legal duo. "Those confessions, the stories I told, they were lies."

Thomas explains that three of the four confessions were false.

"The only true story is the one I wrote in a letter to my wife."

Snyder's head falls to his hands.

The attorney doesn't bother to look at Thomas. He mumbles through his fingers, "And that is?"

"The girl, Thora, died after she jumped out of my car. Everything else I said was a lie."

Snyder and Smith call for the guard to open the cell door, and they leave shaking their heads.

News of Thomas's change of heart spreads quickly through the local law enforcement community.

"He was shaken," Deputy Kennedy tells his buddies when he hears about Thomas's latest story. "McMonigle couldn't believe his wife would do that.

"Almost felt sorry for the schmuck."

CHAPTER 46

February 4, 1946

As his trial begins, Thomas, usually jaunty and even flippant with his armed guards, is losing focus and is distracted. He needs a haircut and is losing weight.

Something's bothering him; is it the trial or Ena's request for a divorce?

He's drumming his fingers on the wooden table in front of him and glancing furtively around the courtroom.

Perhaps, Thomas's tension is because of the trial.

Today, he's going to have to face the parents of the girl he's accused of murdering. But suddenly, the emotions that lined his face vanish. Thomas sits stoically, waiting for the prosecution to open its case by calling Thora's parents to the stand, Frank and Lois Chamberlain.

As expected, it's an emotional afternoon. Frank and Lois describe their little girl as a quiet, home-loving child. At Sunday school, church, and Christian Endeavor — summer religious conferences at Mount Herman — she was a regular.

Lois sobs as she looks at a picture of Thora taken a few weeks before the girl vanished.

"She was always gracious and loving," says Lois to the jury with tears running down her cheeks. "My Thora was always a very honest and trustworthy daughter who was always thoughtful of others."

Frank takes his turn and points out to the jury that Thora

played bass viola in her Sunday school orchestra.

"And she was learning to play the piano," he says.

Frank remembers Thora spent three summers cutting apricots and picking prunes in Victory gardens before she disappeared.

"She had no worries, no enemies," says Frank.

"Do you remember Thora leaving for school, November 2, 1945?" says Stephen Wyckoff, the district attorney.

"Oh yes," says Frank. "She was wearing a new red skirt, a blue sweater, and a white blouse."

Frank pauses and looks directly at the jury.

"Those are the school colors," he explains. "Thora was carrying her books and a cowbell, too. They had a big football game that afternoon. That's why she had the cowbell."

He walks down memory lane with a smile on his face, but Frank's grin soon fades when Stephen Wyckoff shows him a pair of red and blue bobby socks.

"Yes, those seem to be Thora's," Frank nods and whispers. There's a tear in his eye as Frank takes a deep breath and looks at his wife, Lois.

If they didn't before, both realize now that this sorrowful chapter in their lives will never end.

After looking at the red and blue socks, Wyckoff moves Frank's attention to a pair of shoes and some other evidence recovered during the search for Thora.

"Were these Thora's shoes," Wyckoff gently asks. "And these other items; were they Thora's?"

"I can't be sure," Frank says after taking a moment to collect himself. "They appear to be my daughter's as they are similar to those she owned."

"And, what about this compass?"

"Oh," Frank says. He's smiling again, but only for a moment. "That was definitely hers."

Frank turns to the jury again.

"That is a compass I gave to her. It's an old one that I used in school when I was her age."

Then, as he had with Lois, District Attorney Wyckoff requests the defendant stand and asks Frank if he's ever seen Thomas before.

And, just as with Lois, Frank looks sternly toward McMonigle, the man accused of killing his child, and says, "never."

Frank, as had his wife before him, stares at Thomas, searching his face, seeming to ask, "how could you have done this?"

After a quick cross-examination, Frank looks at the jury once again before the judge excuses him.

"I remember I kissed Thora goodbye at the door that morning, And that was the last time I ever saw my little girl."

CHAPTER 47

February 6, 1946

Women, old enough to know better, and girls who don't have the history or maturity to make a rational judgment love Thomas Henry McMonigle. He's said to be embodied with a "strange, persuasive power" over females.

Take, for instance, what happened when he was on trial for beating up his boss, Jack Armstrong, a year ago. This happened while Thomas worked as a San Mateo bus driver.

During that trial, Thomas, facing charges of battery and disturbing the peace, acts as his own attorney after his lawyer, Bush Finnell, withdrew from the case.

With great flair, Thomas calls four women to the stand to speak as character witnesses.

The first three all talk about his "courtesy and service" as a bus driver. The fourth, who lives on North Delaware Street, wrote a letter to the judge.

She wrote, "As I ride these buses from two to four times daily, I have had many opportunities to observe their operation by Mr. McMonigle.

"He has always been most courteous and obliging to all passengers. I hope these few remarks will be considered in his favor."

Those four character witnesses were not alone.

Thomas also submitted a petition — which seems more than ironic now — signed by sixteen Burlingame teenage girls.

It states, "This is to certify that Mr. McMonigle has been most pleasant in his associations with the undersigned high school students and has gone out of his way to be helpful to us.

"We would like to express our appreciation of this helpful and fine attitude."

Well, the testimony as to his character wasn't enough. Thomas was convicted on both charges in connection with his attack on Jack Armstrong.

Yet, beyond that trial, San Mateo Chief of Police Robert O'Brien says what's most important is that there also is a Jekyll and Hyde aspect to Thomas's relationship with women.

"McMonigle has a terrible weakness for women and young girls that arouses the latent evil in him," O'Brien tells a reporter from the San Mateo Times.

Sure, Thomas was able to produce twenty women to speak in his favor. But, O'Brien says there are plenty of Burlingame high school girls who tell a different story.

"There were numerous complaints he tried to pick up high school girls. And the whole thing finally got so bad the kids formed, what they called, a "McMonigle Club.

"Now, some of the girls riding the bus still joked with him. And now and then would arrange a date — which fortunately they did not keep.

"Instead they would watch, and giggle, from a hiding place as McMonigle waited for them a the pre-arranged meeting site."

Most of the seats in the courtroom today are occupied by women. The journalists in attendance note the females are all paying rapt attention to the testimony today from prosecution witnesses.

"Can you believe how many women are here?" One of the reporters in the press section asks a colleague.

"Of course I can; look at the witness list for today. Children."

"So?"

"These women here, they are all looking for sympathetic thrills."

Some of those in the audience do gasp when two young children take the witness stand.

Yvonne Rappe sits on a stack of books in the witness stand today so that she can see over the railing. Eight-year-old Yvonne follows the appearance of her seven-year-old sister, telling the story of what happened to them on November 2, 1945.

And, just like her sibling, Yvonne says they were approached by Thomas just before he's accused of going after Thora Chamberlain.

Both girls tell similar stories about Thomas asking them to drive away with them.

But neither testifies before assuring Judge Atteridge they attend Sunday school every weekend. The girls also tell Atteridge they understand, today more than ever, they must tell the truth.

Older children, teenagers follow the two grammar school children. All five of Thora's closest friends will take the stand today. When asked to identify the man who drove off with Thora to a girl, they all point directly at Thomas.

One of Thora's high school friends, Elaine Scimeca, goes farther when she takes her turn in the witness standing, testifying about her encounter with Thomas.

She tells the judge and jury what she thought of Thomas that day.

"I didn't think he was nice looking at all," she says, "and he had a big nose."

The defense attorneys work with -- no pun intended -- kid gloves during cross examination. Neither wants to be seen as badgering these children.

When asked if she was sure that Thomas drove off with Thora, Elaine adamantly tells defense attorney Stanford Smith that it was him behind the wheel of the 1932 Plymouth.

And Catherine Ban, a senior at Campbell High School, doesn't flinch under gentle cross-examination from Bert Snyder.

"Now, when you saw Thora talking to this man," Bert says and points toward Thomas, "you didn't pay any more attention to him than you did to any other person or object on the street?"

"Yes, I did," replies Catherine.

"Why?"

Catherine takes a moment to look toward the jury. Then, she returns her attention to Bert and smiles.

Describing her grin, a press scribe furiously scribbles, "with demure wisdom," on his notepad.

"When a girl sees another girl talking to a man," Catherine explains, "she always looks to see who the man is."

CHAPTER 48

February 8, 1946

"You would think there was a sale on nylons," a hatless reporter for the Santa Cruz Sentinel-News yells down the line of a payphone to his rewrite man.

His colleague understands immediately.

The war ration on nylons finally lifted, the DuPont company is striving to meet demand but falling far short.

Why, just last August there was a riot of hair-pulling, fist-swinging women when 40,000 of them showed up for a sale, in Pittsburgh, of only 13,000 pairs of stockings.

The courthouse scribe will never find his fedora again. It fell from the reporter's head during the mad scramble of woman outside a set of double courtroom doors.

He's not the only one lucky to escape injury.

This morning, bailiffs and court officers are outnumbered by crazed women, each yearning to get close to Thomas. The women shove and elbow one another as they fight for a seat in the courtroom.

Ever since his photo was published for the first time, women across California have fallen hard for this man, even though he's accused of killing a child.

It's more than Thomas's charisma that's captivated these women. And the frenzy involves more than starstruck females.

All of Santa Cruz is fascinated by this trial. And the fever has only grown since Thomas's trial began.

The story is plastered on the front page, above-the-fold, in papers like The Santa Cruz Sentinel-News. Daily coverage of Thomas's trial trumps even celebrity stories like singer-actress Deanna Durbin giving birth to her first child. The Sentinel-News editors include the delivery of six-pound, five-ounce Jessica Louise as only a one-sentence story for those who care.

And then there's another short story of "red-haired Norma Jean Moore" being granted a "divorce from her radio-announcer husband."

Why this celebrity split? The article from United Press states the straw that broke Norma Jean's back was the night her husband shared their bed with his "man friend" while she was forced to sleep on the floor of their Salt Lake City apartment.

Scintillating right? But still not enough to warrant more than a couple of paragraphs below the fold, just above the announcement of Ileen Lathrop leaving on a "trip across the continent to New York City."

On the other hand, the story of Thomas's trial today will jump from one page to another, along with sidebar stories.

So is this morning's pending stampede of humanity any wonder?'

Doors of the courtroom are shut tight until 9:45 a.m. today, and then all hell breaks loose.

Bailiff Tom Glass opens a single door to let the crowd in, but so many women, and men too, rush forward that both doors nearly burst open.

Every seat inside the courtroom is quickly occupied. Only a few sweaty, bruised combatants are allowed to stand in the back of the room to watch the trial.

But soon, with the command of the judge's gavel, the courtroom is quiet.

First to testify this morning are E.J., agents Fred Elledge and Michael Farrin, and San Mateo's top cop, Chief Robert O'Brien.

Now, Salvatore Guarini, a San Mateo nurseryman, is on the witness stand. He tells the jury how he traded McMonigle a .32

caliber Colt automatic, a gun clip, and a box of eight shells for a .45 Colt automatic.

"We did that deal back, oh, I don't know, sometime in late October," says Salvatore.

The prosecution presents the .32 Colt, which District Attorney Stephen Wyckoff plans to say is the gun used to kill Thora. Along with the gun, the box of a dozen shells is presented as evidence.

The Colt and the shells are passed to the defense table. Thomas's court-appointed attorneys, Stanford Smith and Bert Snyder, examine the evidence.

The courtroom is quiet enough to hear a bullet drop as the spectators and participants soon will.

Thomas looks at the gun and begins blinking rapidly. He starts playing with the bullets, picking up one after another, inspecting the shells, before letting one drop on the wooden table with a vibrating ping that reverberates through the courtroom.

It's enough to make some in the jury box jump.

Thomas shyly looks at his attorneys, then throws a quick smile the way of anyone who cares.

He might have been nervous while examining the weapon Thomas is accused of using to kill Thora.

But, now, with the spotlight on him, Thomas is back to his old self. He looks confident and even cocky as he takes the stand in his own defense. Today, he'll only testify about, and refute, allegations by FBI agents who assert they never threatened him nor offered a deal for his confession or statements about Thora's abduction and death.

Thomas doesn't lose an ounce of his calm demeanor. Although there are sometimes, with a twinkle in his eye, he dances around questions during cross-examination.

In addition, he often apologizes for not remembering the exact dates and times of his conversations with the FBI.

However, Thomas's memory is crystal clear when he claims to recall E.J. offering a deal. Thomas claims E.J. said that he'd try to get Thora's parents to agree to a lesser charge than murder in return for his cooperation.

But Thomas is just getting warmed up. He also testifies that E.J. told him that "the people of Santa Clara are going to erect a memorial for Thora Chamberlain."

And, Thomas says E.J. promised, "if you'll come clean and confess, I'll try to get the trial changed to another county."

CHAPTER 49

February 12, 1946

Thank Heaven there is a doctor in the courtroom. A physician rushes to assist a jury member, Mabel Waters after she collapses in the jury box.

A few hours later, a court reporter tells the press the Watsonville housewife will be okay. However, she won't continue serving, so one of the two alternates, Kenneth Emigh, will take her place.

With that, Emigh, a navy veteran, steps into a trial that's taking new steps to the crazy side of America's justice system.

Remember yesterday when Thomas accused E.J. of offering him a break if only the accused killer would come clean about what he did to Thora?

Well, today, Thomas decides that, yes, he does want to come clean.

Before he is supposed to report to the court, Thomas tells one of the San Quentin guards that he wants to confess.

Now, Thomas says he did murder Thora — at Dunes Beach in San Mateo County — but did not toss her 110-pound body off the 300-foot high cliffs of Devil's Slide into the Pacific Ocean.

Instead, Thomas says he wrapped the girl's body in a blanket, tied it up with rope, and then threw Thora into the water held back by the Crystal Springs Dam at Dunes Beach.

This is the fifth story Thomas has told about Thora's abduction and murder and necessitates the eighth search police have made for her body.

Later, San Mateo County Deputy Sheriff John O'Brien tells the reporters crowded around him by the water that he doesn't put much stock in Thomas's latest story.

"The lake is pretty large," O'Brien says, "and McMonigle gave no indication of the exact spot where the body was thrown."

After pausing to take a breath and allow the various scribes to catch up with pencil and notepad, O'Brien adds, "We don't credit his story very highly."

District Attorney Stephen Wyckoff, who has expressed ultimate confidence in the case he's presenting against McMonigle, also doubts Thomas's new tale.

"His lawyers are probably just trying to get a change of venue," Wyckoff says to Bill Tyree. He's a United Press reporter, recently returned to the States from five years of wartime coverage in the Pacific.

Then, Wyckoff turns to John Keyes of the Call Bulletin and says, "And McMonigle is undoubtedly just trying to gain a couple more months of life."

But, in the courtroom, Thomas says he is serious. And, he wants to change his pleas of not guilty and not guilty by reason of insanity to guilty.

"It's time, to tell the truth," Thomas says as he and his attorneys dictate the new story to a court reporter.

The reporter dutifully taps the keys on his stenotype machine until Thomas runs out of words.

Once finished, Thomas and his court-appointed lawyers review the documents detailing Thomas's new version of the death of Thora Chamberlain.

Thomas sets the papers down on the table before him, smiles, and refuses to sign his name to the documents.

CHAPTER 50

February 17, 1946

While people across the U.S. worry today about the probability of telephone workers striking, they are also being warned of a butter shortage, because farmers are diverting butterfat to milk and cream production instead of butter.

Richard J. Werner, manager of the California Dairy Advisory Board warned yesterday that could result in a two-year "butter famine" up and down the California coastline.

And, it seems like the war will never end.

Alongside coverage of Thomas's trial on the front page of newspapers in California, today is the trial of an Army staff sergeant. He is accused of spying for the Germans in World War II.

Meanwhile, Thomas's trial is due for a new emotional twist as he takes the stand in his own defense this morning.

Now, this is the last thing his attorneys want, but they agree to let him testify. No matter what they think of Thomas, he is their client who argues, quite successfully that since it is his life on the line, Thomas should have every right to take the stand and argue that he is not guilty of Thora's murder.

His attorneys have done all they can. They've tried to foster the proverbial "reasonable doubt" in the minds of the jury.

First, Stanford Smith and Bert Snyder raised the possibility Thora's socks, discovered on the cliffs of Devil's Slide, were thrown there by the girl herself.

After she tossed her socks, the defense team speculates, Thora may have run away barefoot. Perhaps she wanted to get away from her family as much as from Thomas. Who knows?

What about the blood on the grey trousers Thomas buried at the construction yard in Burlingame? Stanford and Bert contend that could have come from anyone. There's no proof, they remind jurors, that the blood on the pants is Thora's blood.

Thomas's attorneys also argue his initial confession actually proves Thomas never intended to end Thora's life. So even if he did kill the girl, Thomas should not be judged guilty of first-degree, premeditated murder.

Bert and Stanford feel they've done their best to protect Thomas's interests, and they might win the case if only their client stays out of the way.

But, to paraphrase an old courtroom cliche, he who represents himself in court has a fool for a client. And boy, does Thomas prove that correct.

Climbing into the witness chair, the spotlight is on Thomas, and he's having the time of his life.

Thomas is in his element this morning. He sits down in the wooden chair beside Judge James L. Atteridge, looks first at the jury with a smile, and then glances toward his attorneys.

He is more than ready.

And then, the court recesses for lunch. Unbelievable.

An hour or so later, his lamb chop lunch fully digested, Thomas is back on the witness stand in the early afternoon.

Confronted with the fact that Thora's body was not found at Dunes Beach even though crews spent hours dragging the lake, Thomas says he has a new story.

He repudiates the story he told theory six days ago. Now, Thomas tells his attorney, Bert Snyder, from the witness stand, Thora's death was accidental.

"The girl didn't want to go back to school. She wanted to stay with me. So we were playing a game. And I was driving quite fast," Thomas says sheepishly.

"Where were you when this was going on," Bert Snyder asks.

"On a country road, I am not sure exactly where," says Thomas. "I was lost. But I think we were about a mile-and-a-half west of Campbell when all of a sudden she got scared and jumped out of the car."

"She jumped?"

"Yeah, exactly right, but I don't know why, except she was scared."

"And what did you do?"

"Oh, I stopped right away, went back, and got her. I put her in the car and did my best to get her to a hospital."

"But you didn't make it?"

"No." Thomas sighs. "I drove as fast as I could, and I was talking to her, trying to keep the girl awake. But she never answered me, and in about five minutes, I realized she was gone. The girl was dead."

"And then?"

"Well, sir, then I pulled the car over and set her body down along the road, very gently. I covered it with leaves, said a prayer, and drove off."

As soon as Bert Snyder looks to the prosecutor's table and says, "your witness," Stephen Wyckoff leaps to his feet like a man possessed. Or at least a district attorney outraged by an accused murderer who's changed his story once too often.

"Mr. McMonigle," says Wyckoff, "how do you expect us to believe this story after all of the other tales you've told that contradict this fairy tale?"

"Oh, it's no fairy tale."

"This one is finally the truth? Please."

"This story is absolutely true, sir. I promise."

"And all of the other stories you told, were what, lies?"

Thomas hangs his head and then looks over to the jury.

"Yes, sir, I am afraid they were lies. But see, I had to do it. I couldn't tell the truth because of you, sir, and others who want to see me hang in Santa Clara County."

"Oh, so we are the ones who should be on trial?"

"I didn't say that." Thomas smiles slyly and looks at the jury again, "but if the shoe fits."

The audience, who's been hanging on Thomas's every word, laughs.

"Uh-huh. Well before the police take me away," says Stephen, "perhaps you can explain the bullet hole we found in your car."

"Oh, that was an accidental shooting," says Thomas.

"Accidental?"

"Yeah, the gun went off by accident, happened several months ago. Back in the summer of last year."

"I see. And what about Thora's socks, the red and blue socks discovered on Devil's Slide?"

"Those socks, if they were found there at all, which I think is a lie; well, they must have been put there by the FBI. They've always wanted to trap me."

"The FBI put them there?"

"Right. Or the agents' statement is just a bald-faced lie."

Stephen paces from the witness stand to the jury box. Looking at the jurors, he says, "You now say the body of Thora Chamberlain —"

"Who died accidentally," states Thomas.

"Yes, who you say died accidentally," says Stephen. "You placed her body along the road, covered it with leaves, said a prayer, and then drove off."

Thomas leans back in the witness chair, crosses his arms over his chest, smiles to the jury, and says, "Yes, that's exactly correct. Couldn't have said it better myself."

Another small wave of laughter sweeps through the court's audience.

Stephen spins to face Thomas.

"Then, Mr. McMonigle, perhaps you could just take us, all of us, to Thora's body tomorrow morning. We could take a drive, all of us together, and you could lead us to the body of Miss Chamberlain.

"What do you say?"

Thomas thinks for a moment, leans forward, and says, "How

'bout throwing in lunch? If you're buyin', I'm flyin'."

People in the audience gasp aloud when Thomas says he will even help authorities find Thora's body. By doing so, he promises to prove the veracity of his latest story, which is the accidental death of Thora Chamberlain.

Superior Judge James L. Atteridge decides he'll load the jury and court officials into a couple of Greyhound buses tomorrow and follow the accused killer's lead.

Sheriff Emig's head drops into his hands. "Good Lord," he mutters.

This trip will involve much more than sandwiches, soft drinks, fresh air for the jury, attorneys, officials, and Thomas's fantasy.

Emig's main concern will be bringing everyone, Thomas included, home alive.

"You know where we're going, don't you?" Emig says to a deputy. When the only response is shoulders shrugging, Emig shakes his head.

Emig knows the spot where McMonigle says the jury will find Thora's body tomorrow is in the same area where Thomas Thurmond and John M. Holmes, accused of kidnapping and killing Brooke Hart, were lynched while a radio audience listened.

Tomorrow, Thomas will be surrounded by even more bodyguards than usual. And, everyone else in the Greyhound convoy will also require armed guards.

Thomas promises, at the end of the day tomorrow, the mystery surrounding the disappearance of Thora Chamberlain will be solved.

Could it be that all this time, Thora's body has been in a shallow grave about five minutes from her home?

CHAPTER 51

February 18, 1946

Thomas changes his mind again. He walks into the courtroom and announces he won't be leading the jury to Thora's shallow grave, after all.

Stanford Smith and Bert Snyder stand together to give the judge this news, but it's Stanford who has to make the announcement.

"And why won't you be making this trip, Mr. McMonigle," asks Judge Atteridge.

"Your honor," answers Attorney Smith.

"No. Mr. Smith, let your client answer the question. Mr. McMonigle, can you explain why you will not lead this trip to find Miss Chamberlain's body. You are aware of the expense and time spent to get this prepared for you, are you not?"

Thomas stands, turns from side to side to make sure everyone's looking at him.

"Your honor." Thomas pauses, enjoying the moment.

"I learned from someone that an armed mob will be waiting for me as soon as I step out of the bus."

"Somebody will be waiting for you? Who would be waiting? Who told you this? Who?"

"I am afraid I cannot say, your honor. But because of a fear for my safety, I just can't do it."

"Be seated," Judge Atteridge says. Then he addresses the jury.

"As there are no more witnesses to present, nor evidence to be seen, I will now deliver the jury's instructions before deliberations begin."

At 3:57 p.m., the jury has its marching orders and leaves the courtroom to begin deciding whether Thomas killed Thora. These five women and seven men know that if they decide he is guilty, they will also be condemning Thomas to die in California's gas chamber.

Can there be any more onerous task facing a human being?

And remember, all District Attorney Wyckoff has presented to the jury is circumstantial evidence. Thora's body has not been found. How can the jury even be sure that the girl is dead?

Once behind closed doors, the jury discusses the evidence. They will vote on a verdict.

The first ballot will settle the question of whether Thomas is guilty of killing Thora. The second ballot asks the jurors if they believe Thomas McMonigle is guilty of first-degree murder.

The vote on both ballots is unanimous.

Their work is finished quickly, and a short thirty-seven minutes after receiving Judge Atteridge's instructions, the jurors return to their places in the jury box.

"Will the defendant rise," asks Judge Atteridge. "The jury has reached its verdict."

Thomas stands and stares ahead stoically as he hears the jury foreman read the verdict.

"Guilty of first-degree murder."

Because there is no recommendation for clemency, Thomas now faces the death penalty.

Hearing those words, Thomas's face hardens. He glares at the jury, the judge, the prosecuting attorneys, and finally, the audience behind him.

For the first time, Thomas's carefree, jovial facade is gone. Now, the courtroom sees the face of a killer.

Judge Atteridge's gavel declares an end to the trial, but he does not dismiss the jury. They'll be needed at one more court hearing and will then decide if Thomas was insane when he murdered Thora Chamberlain.

Atteridge sets February 26 for that trial, which is expected to only last a day.

The court's business for this day is finished.

Reporters at the front of the courtroom wait anxiously for the chamber to empty. As soon as they see a lane open up in the crush of California humanity, the journalists dash to the side of Frank and Lois Chamberlain.

Photographer Murray Fay from the San Francisco Call Bulletin, with his camera, pushes his way to the front and starts taking photos. Alongside him is a colleague and competitor, Seymour Snaer. Bill Regan, a photog with the San Jose News, stands behind the pair taking his pictures from a slightly different angle.

With flashbulbs popping furiously, the reporters jostled and shout for the attention of Frank and Lois Chamberlain.

The first question comes from Bill Gould of the Mercury-Herald. He raises his hand and says, "Reaction Mr. and Mrs. Chamberlain?"

John Keyes, from the Call Bulletin, with his notepad and pencil in one hand, his other hand in the air, shouts, "Will you witness McMonigle's execution?"

Frank holds his right hand up to stop the questions. Friends will later remark Frank and Lois seem to have aged years since the day Thora disappeared.

But still, Frank is steady as he says all he has to say.

"Mrs. Chamberlain and I feel justice has been done."

With that, the reporters respectfully move aside so Frank and Lois can walk out of the court building.

The scribes rush next to Ena McMonigle, Thomas's estranged wife.

Still legally married, while the divorce proceedings continue, Ena only says, "I have my life to live. We will try to forget all of this."

CHAPTER 52

April 19, 1946

The life of a junk dealer can be a lonely existence, but Franklin Hogmire is happy right now just being alone.

Living in a small one-bedroom hotel room with his wife, Lorene, at 397 Fourth Street in Redwood City, is no piece of cake for the thirty-seven-year-old combat veteran. Married not even two years — they tied the knot in November 1944 while Franklin was still in the Army Air Force. The Hogmires landed in San Francisco about eight months ago, and a month later, Franklin was out of the Army.

"Are you ever going to get a job?"

Lorene couldn't let it go. Just twelve weeks into life in the Harrison Hotel and she is going stir crazy. The only time she goes out is at night to work as a waitress at Lucky Joe's Cafe, a couple of blocks away from the hotel, at 188 Fourth Street.

It isn't just being stuck in a hotel room that's getting to Lorene. Her heart aches when she thinks of her ten-year-old daughter Opal Fay who's living in Abilene, Texas, with the girl's father, Lorene's ex-husband.

Franklin fell in love with her at first sight a year ago, but since he was due to go back overseas, that was understandable.

This morning, her thick auburn hair, on top of five-foot-three inches and 167 pounds of curvy womanhood, isn't quite as attractive a package as Franklin remembers. And he's thinking he could use some time alone.

She just doesn't get it, Franklin thinks.

"No, I will not get a job," he says every time Lorene brings up his employment status. "All the time I was in the service, I dreamed of not being bossed around another day of my life. The last thing I need is a new boss."

"You're going to be gone all day again?"

Franklin grunts. The question deserves no more of a reply, he decides.

Franklin's thinking about the "boss" thing. While dressing in his work shirt and blue pants, Franklin decides he's getting plenty of "bossing around" from Lorene, but once he's out of their room, he'll get some peace and quiet. Maybe he'll camp out a day or two on the shore. That's where he's heading this morning.

"So you're going to spend your life living in this room and spending your days looking for junk."

"Yeah, Lorene, I look for junk because I am a junk dealer."

With that, he jams a package of Red Man chewing tobacco in one of his shirt pockets, slams the hotel room door, and walks down to his pickup truck.

A couple of hours later, Franklin's at peace. He should be thinking about how he will come up with a couple of bucks to fill his Ford's gas tank. But right now, he's a man in his own world, a few hundred feet below Devil's Slide, with a warm spring breeze blowing in off the Pacific Ocean.

He's looking for treasure in the sand and between the jagged rocks under his feet. Of course, Franklin's ready to jump out of the way if anything should tumble down off the Slide.

God forbid, he gets buried in one of the Devil's Slide famous landslides. Loud noises make him jump, but since Franklin survived combat in the war, he's not a Nervous Nellie.

In the war, he learned the value of concentrating on the task at hand. Better that than worrying much about the future.

So, six-feet-tall and as lean and trim as he was in the service, Franklin keeps his eyes glued to the ground, pretty much looking for anything that might be worth a few pennies. Maybe something that fell out of a pocket way up there landed down here.

"Good God, there it is!" Franklin can't stop himself from shouting, then looks guiltily over his shoulder to ensure no other treasure hunters are nearby.

Something is sparkling in the sand ahead of him. "Could be jewelry," Franklin mumbles as he tries to avoid tripping and falling flat on his face on the sharp rocks under his feet.

Finally, he's close enough to drop to his knees and starts scooping sand, dirt, and rocks away.

And, then, Franklin finds the source of the reflected sun.

It's a small cross stuck in the sand. Franklin moves closer and sees something else flickering in the sun.

A ring! Franklin's thinking he might have just hit the junkyard jackpot.

He sticks his hand in the dirt, going for the jewelry, and comes out with a human hand.

"Jesus," Franklin shouts as he leaps to his feet, still holding on to the hand of a corpse. "Good Lord!"

Since he didn't let go of the dead person's hand, Franklin pulls the body attached to the hand partway out of its shallow grave.

Trembling, Franklin slips and falls backward. His hat lands behind him.

Instinctively, Franklin grabs for it before looking closer at the decomposed body of a woman, a Negro woman, he's found under the cliffs of Devil's Slide.

CHAPTER 53

Out of his mind with shock and adrenaline, Franklin pushes sand back over the woman's body, replaces the cross, and then scrambles back up Devil's Slide faster than he thought possible.

He yanks the driver's side door open and hops into his beat-up 1936 Ford Coupe. Breathing like a man who'd just climbed a 350-foot cliff, which Franklin, of course, had, he slams the rust bucket's transmission into gear.

Then, without wasting time trying to catch his breath, Franklin slams the coupe's door shut twice to keep it closed. Sweat steaming down his forehead makes his rugged face look like a map of the Great Rivers of The World.

Franklin doesn't even mop his brow. Instead, he drives like a man who has just found a dead body -- which again, he has -- to the nearest payphone to call the police.

"Down to my last nickel and this is how I'm going to spend it," Franklin mutters as he curses his luck.

Minutes after the dispatcher who takes Franklin's call hangs up, E.J. is notified that a body had been discovered not from where Thomas said he'd tossed Thora's corpse.

"What the hell's this place? Disposal Cliff?" E.J. shakes his head and then quickly calls his men into action.

E.J. and his men run like the wind into one of their FBI-issued cars, speed to San Quentin, check Thomas out for the day, and put the gas pedal to the metal to race to Devil's Slide.

"So you think this could be her?"

E.J. looks over his shoulder at Thomas, wedged between two other FBI agents in the back seat.

"Think this might be Thora?"

It's about the hundredth time one of the agents has asked the question, and for the hundredth time, Thomas shrugs and says, "Yeah, I think it could be. It probably is."

"Or maybe just another wild goose chase," says one of the agents sitting beside Thomas.

"Well, at least it's a body," says the agent jammed into the other side of the back seat.

Thomas, residing on Death Row in San Quentin since March 5, has come up with one story after another about what happened to Thora.

He's also been devouring the maximum-security prison's law library. "I'm working on my appeal," Thomas says to a fellow killer on Death Row.

"We logged one-thousand miles on your other wild goose chases," says one of Thomas's bookend agents, the beefy suit sitting on the right.

Thomas smiles and shrugs.

"But this time will be different," says the agent on the left.

"Absolutely," says Thomas.

Maybe he's finally telling the truth.

Thomas has a hangdog look of a guilty man on his face today. E.J. has to admit this is different than the other three times or the multiple January excursions to find Thora's body.

To kill time, one of the agents in the back grabs a newspaper. He starts reading about the rescue of a famous actress during the shooting of a movie.

"Want to hear what happened to Greer Garson the other day?" says the agent, talking across Thomas to his backseat partner.

"Can we stop you?"

The agent with the newspaper laughs and begins reading aloud.

"Vincent Sollecito, a handsome 35-year-old fishing boat skipper who picks up extra money working as a Hollywood movie extra, tells reporters today that he's still dreaming about yesterday's rescue of Greer Garson.

"Vincent was working as an extra on a seaside move set when he saw an eight-foot wave knock the picture's leading lady off a rock. Vincent waded into the water and grabbed the actress.

"'You're a hero, Vincent,' says one of the first reporters on the scene, a scribe from United Press.

"'No, not me,' says Vincent.

"'But you rescued Greer Garson.'

"'Yeah, but there was nothing to it. I just waded out and scooped her up,' says Vincent.

"'It was as easy as fishing a slippery sardine out of a bucket.'"

"He makes it sound easy, but Vincent saved the academy award winner's life," says the narrating agent.

The agent continues, "It says here that Garson is hospitalized today and probably will stay there for several days. She suffered abrasions on her body, cuts on her legs, and is suffering from shock."

E.J.'s been following the story from the front seat. He doesn't turn as he asks, "And what about this guy, Vincent?"

"Oh, Vincent? He's in a dream, boss."

"Listen to this. 'I've often pictured carrying Greer Garson in my arms,' Vincent says, 'but I never thought I would do it.'"

"Isn't that a great story?" the agent says. "I love happy endings."

He rolls the newspaper into a tube and whacks Thomas over the head.

"Is your story gonna have a happy ending today, Thomas?"

The FBI man driving the Ford snorts and enters the conversation for the first time.

"Happy ending? Yeah. When they turn on the gas, that will make me happy, and it sure as hell will be the end. Finally."

CHAPTER 54

After another hour in the car, the agents and Thomas pull off the road and onto the beach. Looking to the north, they can see Devil's Slide. So they are not far from where Thomas said, the first time, that he killed Thora and tossed her body into the Pacific Ocean.

A man, about six-feet-tall, is waiting for them, wearing blue work pants and a khaki work shirt.

The shirt has two pockets in the front, one holding a daily ration of Red Man. The agents can see the back of the man's shirt is soaked with sweat.

The guy's moping his brow with a bandana, his hat in his other hand.

Two motorcycle cops are standing beside him.

E.J. walks up to the cops and points to Franklin. "Him?"

The cops nod and step aside.

With a quick handshake, E.J. introduces himself to Franklin.

"So you were down here; why?"

"Looking for junk."

"Junk?"

"Yeah," says Franklin. This isn't the first time some college egghead-looking guy has questioned his profession. "That's what I've been doing ever since I got out of the Army."

Franklin shrugs. "I find it, and I sell it."

"But this time," E.J. says, "you found something more?"

Franklin nods and puts his hat back on his head. "Oh, I'd say so, buddy."

"Okay," says E.J., and he signals to his team he's ready to move on. One of the other agents takes E.J.'s place in the conversation. He's got a pad and pencil prepared to take a more official statement.

The motorcycle cops mount up and ride off just as the coroner's meat wagon drives up.

"So, what's the story now, Thomas?" E.J. takes off the handcuffs that have been holding Thomas's arms in front of his body.

One of the other agents looks at E.J. with a raised eyebrow.

"Don't need the cuffs now," E.J. says. "I doubt he's going to run away from the four of us."

"Wish he'd try," mutters the agent who's thinking about taking off his shoes to knock the sand out.

But despite the agent's show of impatience, E.J. and his men realize they've really got something this time. If nothing else, it is the body of a woman, decomposed, with most of its features eaten by every crab on the beach. But, it still could be recognizable.

The agents, Franklin, and Thomas, walk for about a hundred yards.

Thomas stops.

"Over there." Thomas gestures toward a mound of sand.

E.J. looks at Franklin, who nods his head in agreement.

"That's where you'll find Thora," Thomas whispers.

The agents, led by E.J., move quickly to what does appear to be a makeshift, shallow grave. Thanks to Franklin, most of the body is out of the sand.

The four agents look to their boss for leadership and guidance because it looks like, for once, Thomas is telling the truth.

"Take it easy," says E.J. "Remember, we've probably got a murder crime scene here."

The other four agents get down on their knees and start scooping sand with their hands. E.J. takes the small cross as evidence. He looks back at Thomas to make sure he doesn't get any wild ideas about escaping. But Thomas is even more interested than the FBI as to what might be buried in the sand.

"Oh, Christ!" An agent shouts. He stands up, looking for E.J.

"We've got her boss," says another agent.

They make way for E.J. Now, he's on his knees and, with his fingertips, moves sand off the face of what sure as hell is a human corpse buried in the sand.

The other four agents, and Thomas, are behind E.J. and Franklin standing back out of the way.

But, each is looking over their boss's shoulder for a glimpse of the body of Thora Chamberlain.

However, just like light is faster than sound, the unmistakable stench of death is what hits the men first.

"Good God," says an agent. He rips a handkerchief out of his jacket pocket and slaps it across his nose and mouth.

The others follow suit and back away. Thomas has no handkerchief, nor does he seem bothered by the stench of a dead, decomposing body.

He actually moves closer.

"Oh, shit," says Thomas.

E.J. stands and grabs his prisoner by the lapels of his San Quentin jacket.

"Yeah, oh shit," says E.J. "I don't have a clue who that is, but it isn't Thora, is it?"

Thomas shakes his head. The other agents move closer, each wondering to a man, what the hell now?

Thomas is focused on the body, frozen in thought, forgetting for a moment that he's surrounded by federal agents.

Finally, he looks up at E.J. Thomas's confidence is shattered. He's trying to make his mouth work, and though his lips are moving, no words are coming out.

Until he says, "No, that ain't the kid. That ain't Thora."

Thomas looks from one agent to the other and says, "That's Dorothy."

CHAPTER 55

Thomas admits he murdered the twenty-three-year-old woman. But it isn't the FBI's case. So, E.J. hands Thomas and the dead woman over to the local cops.

"Tell me about this woman you say you killed."

"She worked at a restaurant in the neighborhood, lives, or lived on Howard Street," Thomas says to Sheriff James McGrath.

The sheriff doesn't blink but instead locks onto Thomas with his eyes, refusing to let him go.

"We fought because we'd both been drinking."

Thomas sighs.

"Drinking and fighting. That is just what we did."

"How'd she die?"

"She had a knife," Thomas smiles as if remembering a pleasant memory. "Dorothy always carried a knife. When she pulled it on me, I took it away and stabbed her with it."

"How many times?"

Thomas sighs. "Oh, I don't know. It was a long time ago, back in October, last year, I think."

"Where's the knife now?"

"You have it."

"What?"

"Yeah, the knife you took from me when the FBI arrested me."

Sheriff McGrath nods his head.

"That's the knife," says Thomas.

"Why'd you do it?"

Thomas opens his shirt for McGrath.

"See here, and here," Thomas says as he points to scars on his chest. "These are from the Negro bitch. That's what she did to me before I got the knife away."

McGrath looks at the two-way mirror. He knows his men are paying rapt attention, and the secretary banging out Thomas's confession on her typewriter hasn't missed a word, either.

"Okay, so you kill Miss Jones."

"Dorothy."

"Right. Dorothy. She's dead. You're sure of it. What happens next?"

Thomas rubs his dry lips. He'd given anything for even a sip of water.

"Well, what would anybody do? I know I have to get rid of the body."

"So?"

"So, I drive out to Devil's Slide and toss her body over the edge."

Thomas shrugs. He looks at McGrath, begging for understanding.

"You gotta know I didn't want to do it, but she pulled the knife on me. She stabbed me. What was I going to do?"

"Jesus," mutters McGrath. He waves a hand to his deputies on the other side of a two-way mirror, and they come in to lead Thomas away.

It doesn't take long for the police and sheriff's deputies to find a couple of Dorothy's friends. Vannie Brooks and Marie Dorsey live in the same hotel that Dorothy called home.

A few threats later, they agree to come downtown to identify the dearly departed, Miss Jones.

"It's her," says Vannie after the coroner pulls the white sheet off Jones's face, and another shows what's left of the clothes found with the corpse, along with a leather scabbard that was on Dorothy's leg.

"That's Dorothy," says Marie.

Walter Moore, one of the deputies playing muscular bookends for the witnesses, says, "You're positive? She's not much more than a skeleton."

"Oh yeah," answers Marie. "See those gold teeth? And the grey skirt and jacket? That's Dorothy."

Vannie nods in agreement. "That knife case, that's what she always had strapped to her thigh. Always carried a knife on her for protection."

"Did you ever see your friend, Dorothy, with this guy," Deputy Jack O'Brien says as he shows Marie and Vannie one of Thomas's photos.

The witnesses glance at the photo, at each other, then back to the deputy. "No doubt about it," says Vannie. "Saw them together back in the fall."

"Must have been October," says Marie, "about a week, maybe ten days before Halloween."

"What were they doing?"

"What else?" Vannie smiles at Marie. "Getting drunk."

"And they'd soon be fighting," says Marie.

Vannie looks at O'Brien and then Moore.

"You had to figure it'd end up like this."

Marie says, "Most always does."

CHAPTER 56

April 20, 1946

E.J.'s team is working in the space that functions as their squad room one last time. As far as they are concerned, the Thora Chamberlain murder case is closed.

"Suspect arrested, booked, convicted," says one of the agents,

"And soon to be gassed in the chamber," replies another of the young men wearing black suits, white shirts, and narrow black ties.

They've all got their fedoras on their heads, packing up the last of the files for shipment back to FBI headquarters in Washington D.C.

The only agent not threatened with the danger of a paper cut is E.J. He's in what passes for his office. Looks the same, except for one change.

For this final conversation, E.J. sits in a wooden chair looking at a county sheriff's inspector, making himself comfortable behind his former desk. And the FBI's kidnapping expert is letting his old friend lead the conversation.

"Hey, look at this here," says Inspector Al Corrasa from the Alameda County Sheriff's Office. He points to the front page of the Daily Review. "Our old buddy 'Peek-A-Boo' Pennington's in hot water, again."

"No kidding? What'd William do now?"

Both men are going to enjoy this conversation. William Pennington is a private eye that puts food on his table by taking bedroom black-and-whites of cheating husbands and wives caught with their pants and panties down.

"Divorce work can be very lucrative," says E.J. with a knowing smile. "You're just going to want to take a shower after every job."

"I'll give you that one," Al chuckles. "But now there's a hotel in Sacramento that says Peek-A-Boo kicked down one of their doors to snap a photo of that bandleader Ray Wade doing it with Ann Harris."

"No!" E.J. leans forward.

Ray Wade's country swing band is one of E.J.'s favorites. The Rhythm Riders always bring huge crowds to dance halls in the San Francisco Bay Area. E.J. is never alone in finding a young lady to do the push-and-pull four-step to the Riders' hit song "You Can't Give Me Back My Heart."

"Oh, but here they quote Peek-A-Boo as saying, 'I knocked on the door and Wade let me in. No door was smashed. It was all friendly.'"

"Oh, I'll bet it was friendly." E.J. laughs as his colleague in crime-fighting lays the newspaper down on his desk. "That's why there were so many clothes on the floor."

Al and E.J. share a laugh.

But then they get serious, in a collegial way.

"My men are about ready to leave," says E.J. "Anything else you need from us?"

Al snorts. "Oh gee whiz, what else could you possibly do after dumping the beach babe hot potato in our laps?"

"Hey, we thought McMonigle was taking us to our victim's body."

"But instead, it turned out to be ours."

"At least it is now; our case is closed."

Al leans back in E.J.'s — now his — swivel chair.

"Well, there's not much work to do," says Al.

"No?"

"Nope. McMonigle already confessed to killing this Negro woman, even gave us her name, Dorothy Rose Jones."

E.J. waits for another shoe to drop.

Al leans forward in the swivel chair, his elbows on the desk.

"Says he picked her up from a restaurant in San Francisco, they got into an argument, one thing led to another, and he killed her."

"Sounds pretty matter of fact."

"Oh yeah. This character is one cold fish."

E.J looks back and sees his crew is just about done packing, so he stands up, stretches, and reaches his right hand forward to give Al a final handshake goodbye.

On his way out the door, E.J. turns back in Al's direction.

"So that's it? Is your case closed too? No further investigation?"

"Right. As long as the supreme court doesn't overturn McMonigle's conviction for the Chamberlain killing, our district attorney says he's not going to bother prosecuting the Negro's killing."

E.J. turns to face Al full on.

"What about the woman's family? Don't they deserve to see McMonigle stand trial?"

Al shrugs his broad shoulders but doesn't break eye contact with E.J.

"You know, Al, I don't think McMonigle is the only cold fish in this county."

CHAPTER 57

April 24, 1946

Talk about a hot potato. Today, there's a new problem. Lorene Hogmire has vanished.

"Lorene tells me she has today and tomorrow off from Lucky Joe's so I tell her to come out to Devil's Slide with me," says Franklin. "She's been gripping for days about being left home alone. Ever since the county hired me to keep looking for Thora Chamberlain's body, Lorene has been on my back."

Now, he has a job. Franklin's a county employee. He soon discovers, however, a semi-steady paycheck is not enough to make Lorene any happier.

Once he leads the FBI to Dorothy's body, Franklin becomes the latest folk hero in this part of California. Now it's true he didn't find Thora's body. But this time, even without horseshoes or hand grenades, close is good enough.

San Mateo county bosses quickly sign Franklin to a deal to keep searching around Devil's Slide for the body of Thora Chamberlain.

That means money will be coming into his cookie jar even if he doesn't find the kid.

"But Lorene still isn't content because she is still left home alone," says Franklin.

San Mateo County Deputy John "Jack" O'Brien listening to Franklin slowly nods his head in agreement.

"So today, I finally agree to take her out with me," Franklin says, "and look what happens."

The second deputy in the interview, Deputy Adolph Waldeck, shifts forward in his wooden chair, puts his elbows on the table, separating him from Franklin.

"And what happened, Mr. Hogmire?"

"Well, I take her out to Devil's Slide," says Franklin, "and she's jabbering the whole way, complaining that I didn't ask for enough money to do this, and says we should get some huge reward if we find the body of this kid. You know, blah, blah, blah."

The deputy nods his agreement again.

"So you get out there, you and the missus, and what happens next?"

"Okay. So we get there. I tell Lorene to park her ass in the Coupe. Of course, she complains, and says she wants to go down the cliffs with me."

"And you say?"

"I couldn't help laughing. She's wearing slacks, a suit coat and white sandals. How far do you think she'd get dressed like that?"

"So you leave Lorene in the car."

"Hey, she has her smokes and a bottle of Four Roses. Should be happy, I figure. If nothing else, I got her out of the hotel room.

"'Don't move,' I say, 'I'll be back for lunch.' Then I hop out of the car, tie a couple hundred-foot of rope onto the bumper of the Ford.

"I shimmy down the drop, hundreds of feet down, and start searching again. Hoping I will get lucky.

"And I was damn glad for some peace and quiet if you know what I mean."

"Sure," says O'Brien. "Find anything?"

Franklin sips at his lukewarm coffee, provided free of charge by the sheriff's office. Only fitting, Franklin thinks; after all, I am one of them now.

"Nah, nothing. So I climb back up to the car around noon. Figure Lorene's talked herself out by now, at least she's had some whiskey for company, and we could eat the sandwiches we brought with us."

"And?"

"And, she's gone. The car's locked tight, but Lorene is nowhere to be seen."

"What?"

"Yeah, I know that's just what I said. Lorene's gone. Probably walking, I figure. She bores easily, you know."

"So, did you look for her?"

"Look for her? Look for Lorene? Nope. Figured she could go on her merry way if that's what she wanted to do. Lorene could walk home as far as I was concerned."

Franklin pauses and looks to O'Brien and Waldeck for understanding. Receiving none, he continues, "Besides, I was hungry. Damn hungry."

"You eat lunch," Deputy Waldeck says after writing a few more notes in the book in front of him, "and then you look for your wife?"

Franklin drums his finger on the table. "Well, no. Not exactly."

"So, what exactly did you do?"

"I took a nap."

"Of course, and when you woke up?"

"I climbed back down that rope and went back to work."

Deputy O'Brien puts down his pencil and stares at Franklin. "Your wife is missing for God knows how long, maybe hours. But you don't look for her; you go back to work."

"Yeah, well, you gotta know Lorene like I know her. And then you'd understand."

"Okay, Mr. Hogmire. How long did you stay at Devil's Slide."

"I climbed up for the last time at about, oh, it must have been 4:30."

"And still no sign of Lorene?"

"Right. So I called you guys."

The deputy looks at his notes.

"But it says here you didn't call us until 7:30. Three hours later."

"Yeah, that's right."

"You waited three more hours?"

"Well, you know I'd work hard all day. Not easy climbing up and down Devil's Slide. Had to eat dinner."

O'Brien and Waldeck look at each other and silently agree. It's time to call Chief Deputy Sheriff Walter Moore.

CHAPTER 58

Chief Deputy Sheriff Walter Moore and his wife are sitting on the sofa, hand-in-hand. Smiles of pure contentment on their faces as they listen to one of their favorite radio programs.

A perfect evening, Walter's thinking, and then the phone rings. His wife looks at him. By mutual agreement, she gets up to answer.

After a quick conversation, Moore's wife hands the receiver to the deputy sheriff. He listens for a few minutes, grunts a reply, and hangs up.

"Another body," Mrs. Moore asks. Somehow, she just knows.

"Yeah," her husband mutters. "Mrs. Hogmire."

"Who?"

"Franklin Hogmire's wife."

Mrs. Moore is still puzzled.

"You remember. The guy who thought he found Thora Chamberlain's body. But it turned out to be the skeleton of a woman, a waitress."

"Ah, yes."

"I've got to get out there right now," Moore tells his wife. "The last thing we need is for the wife of the man who found that Negro woman's body to be discovered dead by some hayseed."

"You mean another junk man?"

"Exactly."

Driving into the sheriff's office along the north coastline, Moore decides the fog's too thick to be climbing up Devil's Slide to look for Mrs. Hogmire.

"Instead," he explains to Waldeck and O'Brien, "we're going

door to door along the coastline and talk to anyone who might have seen the woman."

For the next five hours, Waldeck, O'Brien, and Moore visit every beer-soaked roadside tavern and greasy-spoon restaurant along the north coastline.

"Say 'hello' to number twenty," says Waldeck.

Pushing the door open and leading the way, he says to O'Brien, "Your turn." Moore is standing alongside his deputies, offering moral support, leadership, and muscle when needed.

They've gone through this routine so many times tonight, they could do it in their sleep. And all three men are afraid they will.

"Fine," says O'Brien. He pushes a photo toward a small, thin man washing bar glasses. "This woman. You see here in here tonight?"

The man shakes his head, turns, and starts to walk to a customer who needs a beer.

"Hey!" Moore reaches over the bar and grabs the bartender before he can take another step. "This is important. Her name is Lorene Hogmire. She has auburn hair, stands about five-three, and weighs 167."

"Was wearing light blue slacks, white sandals, and a grey sport coat," says O'Brien.

He's on his last nerve.

O'Brien, Waldeck, and Moore have stopped at every roadside tavern and restaurant along the north coastline.

They've asked every barkeeper and cashier who has poured a drink or slung some hash tonight if they have seen Lorene. So their patience is running as thin as the catsup offered to a customer.

"Who?"

"Hogmire. Lorene Hogmire," says Moore.

"Funny name," says the bartender. "I've heard it before but ain't seen her. Not in here."

As they walk out of the tavern, Moore looks at the watch on his left arm. Just about one a.m., Moore calls an end to the nighttime search.

"Tomorrow," he says, "we'll round up a posse just like we did in the old days, before the war. We'll go up on the cliffs tomorrow when this damn fog clears. If Mrs. Hogmire is up there, we'll find her."

CHAPTER 59

April 25, 1946

Waldeck and O'Brien are exhausted. Neither of them got more than three hours of sleep last night. But, being war veterans, they've survived worse, much worse.

First, today, they went to the Harrison Hotel again. Of course, they'd stopped there last night to see if Lorene had turned up. But since she hadn't come home last night, Moore told his men to stop at the hotel first thing this morning.

He wanted to be sure Lorene wasn't asleep in her own bed while he was leading a posse to Devil's Slide.

"Still haven't seen her," says the hotel clerk. The same guy was behind the desk last night, so he was just about as tired as Waldeck and O'Brien.

And his fuse was just as short.

"You're sure?"

The clerk purses his lips and holds his temper. After all, he is talking to the law. So instead of the first thing on his mind, he says, "I was here all night, deputy. If Lorene Hogmire came through this lobby, I would be the first to know."

Waldeck and O'Brien hit Lucky Joe's next.

"I understand Lorene had yesterday off, and she's not expected in today," says O'Brien to the cashier. "But we gotta check. Have you seen Lorene Hogmire this morning?"

"No, honey, I told you," the cashier says and leans close to O'Brien. "She ain't been in. And I don't expect Lorene in until tomorrow."

O'Brien tips his cap to say "thanks, see you later" before walking out to the squad car.

Waldeck is waiting behind the wheel. As usual, he's reading a newspaper. O'Brien opens the passenger door, slides in, and Waldeck points to a photo of some women getting off a ship in San Francisco.

"Look at this," he says, "war brides, more than 400 of them, all from Australia and New Zealand. One of them knit herself a stars-and-stripes sweater, it says here, while she was coming up from 'down under.'"

Waldeck looks at his partner. It doesn't take a cop to read O'Brien's face.

"Let me guess," says Waldeck. "Another goose egg?"

"You got it, buddy. Just another load of lousy," O'Brien says.

Waldeck sighs and whacks the steering wheel with his rolled-up copy of The Times.

"Okay. Fine. We ain't gonna be able to do this the easy way," he says.

"Yeah. On to Devil's Slide."

So here they are, about an hour later, following Chief Deputy Sheriff Moore up a winding path to the cliff where Franklin says he last saw his wife, Lorene.

"Well, at least the fog's gone," says Waldeck. He lifts his cap and wipes his brow.

O'Brien nods. "And at least nobody's gonna tell us 'nope,' today and slam a door in our faces."

Waldeck laughs. "Yeah, you would have thought we were trying to sell vacuum cleaners last night."

While O'Brien, Waldeck, and Moore lead their posse of close to thirty volunteers searching for Lorene Hogmire, another search party is looking for Thora Chamberlain's body.

District Attorney Leonard Avilla earlier this morning stood before his assembled law enforcement troops.

"I am confident McMonigle was telling the truth the first time, and he will lead us to Miss Chamberlain's body today," he says.

So with Thomas Henry McMonigle leading them, they scramble up and down the sides of hills and mountains in a 100-mile area of Santa Cruz County.

Stopping to catch their breath, the hard, cold eyes of every deputy in the search effort stare at Thomas.

He wipes his brow, turns to DA Avilla, and says, "I could have sworn this is where I threw Thora into the Pacific.

"But I just don't recognize a damn thing. Sorry."

The end of the day is just as dispiriting for Moore's team.

"No sign of her," he says to a dispatcher over a radio-telephone in his car.

"Don't let Hogmire out of your sight. I need to talk to him ASAP."

CHAPTER 60

April 26, 1946

U.S. Secretary of State James F. Byrnes, appointed by President Truman last July, deals with a considerable challenge today. How will he convince his counterparts in France, Great Britain, and the Soviet Union to sign the final peace treaties to end WWII?

The shooting may have stopped last year, but the three nations still need to gather in Paris to ratify accords covering Italy, Finland, and the Axis countries of the Balkans.

Byrnes fears France is floating into the Soviet Union's orbit, or so concludes Ray Tucker, a columnist for the McClure Newspaper Syndicate.

However, World War II veteran Franklin Hogmire couldn't care less. He worries only about his wife, Lorene. At least that's what he says to anyone willing to listen.

Franklin's saying today that ironically, while he was searching for the body of Thora Chamberlain, his wife, Lorene, may have been kidnapped.

Franklin's not the only one fearing abduction.

A county-wide search has been going on ever since Lorene vanished from the couple's Ford Coupe, Wednesday. Volunteers are working alongside police officers, including the Hogmire's landlady, the operator of the Harrison Hotel, none other than Mrs. R.C. Bayhi.

She and other volunteers, along with police tracking dogs, made a thorough search of the coast side area Wednesday night and Thursday.

Mrs. Bayhi and the others logged plenty of miles as they traveled side roads and checked again with every home, tavern, and restaurant they came across.

But, today, Mrs. Bayhi has to admit it was all for naught.

"We discovered nothing," she tells a reporter from The Times. "Not a single clue."

Mrs. Bayhi isn't the only mystified member of the search effort. Franklin can't figure it out either.

Especially troubling is that he says there are no footprints in the gravel by their car, which was parked atop Devil's Slide.

And Lorene's handbag was still in the car, which was locked tight.

So what happened to her?

Could Lorene have been kidnapped?

Maybe.

But Franklin hangs on to a slim threat of hope today.

"She might have gone to Wichita Falls, Texas," he says to Mrs. Bayhi. "Maybe she wanted to visit her nine-year-old daughter."

Mrs. Bayhi raises her eyebrows.

"Yeah, another child from another marriage," he says.

Franklin shrugs.

"But," he says, "she didn't have her purse, so Lorene couldn't have had enough money for a bus ticket to Texas."

Still, Lorene does have a sister in Wichita Falls and another sister in Oklahoma City.

"How could she go to either place, though," Franklin wonders, "without her handbag?"

Mrs. Bayhi agrees with Franklin. She says Lorene never would have left the car without her purse.

Mrs. Bayhi, however, completely contradicts Franklin's assertion that Lorene was begging to go to Devil's Slide. Mrs. Bayhi insists Lorene never wanted to go to the cliff to assist Franklin in searching for Thora's corpse.

"Lorene begged him not to continue the search," Mrs. Bayhi says to a nearby police officer.

"She'd been sick and was very upset over her husband going

up on Devil's Slide, searching for that body."

Just as Franklin puts another plug of tobacco in his mouth, a sheriff's deputy approaches.

"We've got news, Mr. Hogmire. Just got a call from someone who's seen a woman who looks just like your wife."

Franklin jumps to his feet.

"Where? When?"

"The caller says a woman fitting Mrs. Hogmire's description was eating a meal yesterday at the Doll House Cafe on El Camino in San Carlos.

"We've got a team of investigators headed there now."

Franklin jumps in his Ford Coupe to get to the Doll House Cafe as quickly as possible.

But, as he shifts into third gear, Franklin wonders, how the hell did she think she was going to pay for the meal?

CHAPTER 61

May 2, 1946

Thomas is hard at work again today, going through the law books provided to inmates at San Quentin. He's becoming quite the jailhouse lawyer as he works on an appeal of his murder conviction.

"Ever hear of 'corpus delicti'" he asks a fellow inmate. Thomas is surrounded by more books than he's read in his lifetime. It's like a fortress of knowledge.

Silence being the only response to his question, Thomas continues.

"Well, look here. Corpus delicti. It's Latin and means concrete evidence of a crime. Like, for instance, a corpse. A dead body."

Only stony silence is heard from the other side of the large wooden table that's got generations of inmate initials carved in the mahogany.

"A dead body. Concrete evidence," Thomas says again, but louder.

The inmate's eyes across the table have transformed from sleepy to a stone-cold glare. Even ignorant criminals don't like to be reminded of their lack of intelligence.

Thomas misses the signal. He pounds his fist on the table and, with a smile of pure joy lighting his face, says, "Guess what was missing from my trial?"

The other inmate only shrugs.

"A corpse! Concrete evidence!" Thomas leans back in his wooden chair and crosses his arms over his chest. "That's just what my trial didn't have."

Thomas drums his fingers on the table, barely able to contain himself.

"I'm going to win this appeal."

At the same time, San Mateo County Deputy Sheriff Jack O'Brien and Orville Hanson from the county forestry department are rappelling down the cliffs of Devil's Slide.

Sheriff James McGrath focuses on finding Lorene Hogmire — dead or alive — with as much vigor as Thomas is expending on his appeal for freedom.

Very few volunteers have continued into this second week to look for Lorene. But McGrath continues to commit more than a fair share of his people to find the woman who vanished from her car atop Devil's Slide.

O'Brien and Hanson have been assigned to the search every day since Lorene went missing. The pair hasn't spent a day on concrete roads for the past two weeks other than driving every day to and from Devil's Slide.

Orville says, "Ever think you'd be back on a rope after coming home from the war?"

O'Brien looks at his companion with a stare that could freeze the Pacific's saltwater.

"This isn't law enforcement," O'Brien complained to a deputy at roll call this morning. "You could round up a bunch of boy scouts to do what I'm doing."

But today, he and Orville are doing it again. Dropping down the cliffs of Devil's Slide.

"This is about where Hogmire found that woman's body," Orville announces on a cliff as they prepare to drop another 200 feet to the next precipice.

Only a few moments later, their feet are on a lower cliff.

Just as Thomas and his fellow inmate are staring into each other's eyes, Orville and O'Brien find a white sandal.

They look at each other with raised eyebrows.

"Could be close," O'Brien whispers.

Why he's speaking quietly, neither man knows. But the

modulation of his voice fits the mood.

O'Brien's in the lead again as he and Orville walk another twenty paces. At their twenty-first pace, Orville inhales so sharply O'Brien stops and looks back at his partner.

"Damn," the deputy mutters, and both men kneel to get a closer look at what Orville was the first to spot.

O'Brien says, "It's a grey coat."

"Lady's sport coat," says Orville.

Both men stand and brush the dirt off their pants.

O'Brien checks his watch and sees it is about 2 p.m. and they have yet to break for lunch.

Instead of working on the sandwiches in their backpacks, O'Brien returns the watch to his pocket and they begin walking again.

Slowly.

Picking their way through brush and trees, they're creeping downhill, examining every inch of the ground.

Neither wants to take a chance of missing a clue. Yet, O'Brien and Orville are also afraid of what must await them.

It's challenging work. Both men are dirty and sweaty, with beads of perspiration running into their eyes.

And then, just as their concentration slips, they stop again.

For a moment, both men forget how to breathe.

Looking up at O'Brien and Orville, her battered, broken body tangled in a mess of brush and small trees, is none other than Mrs. Franklin (Lorene) Hogmire.

Orville keys his walkie-talkie to relay the news back to headquarters.

"Well," sighs O'Brien. "Guess we can forget about the Doll House Cafe."

CHAPTER 62

By the time O'Brien and Orville climb back up to the peak of Devil's Slide, hundreds of people are gathered to watch the recovery of Lorene's body.

It's never easy to do their work with a mob of onlookers staring over their shoulders. But, police officers, fire warden's deputies, and sailors from Point Montara naval base use a spiderweb network of ropes and pulleys to slowly lift Lorene's broken body from her temporary resting place.

"Can you believe this crowd?" Orville says. He forces the words out while gasping for air.

O'Brien's legs quiver like they're made of pudding. His hands are on his hips, and he, too, is fighting for whatever oxygen is available.

Reporters are everywhere, along with their photographers. However, not every journalist in California is here. Plenty more are working in Beverly Hills today.

Paul "Pauley" Gibbons, one of the region's most notorious gamblers, once thought of as the toughest guy in the rackets in the West, was executed by three guys in a black Cadillac last night.

Gibbons's death is only the second murder reported in the exclusive community since Beverly Hills was incorporated thirty-two years ago.

So the pack of scribes here at Devil's Slide could be worse, but it's plenty bad enough if you're a cop trying to deal with the recovery of a woman's body found at the bottom of a 300-foot drop.

But what's really setting O'Brien and Orville back is the throng of average Joes, along with their wives and kids who have turned out in the dark of night.

"Close to midnight," says O'Brien. "Shouldn't these people be home in bed?"

Orville nods his agreement and then is blinded by a blast of a photographer's flashbulb. The reporters begin shouting questions to the men who found the body of Lorene Hogmire.

"What was it like finding her corpse?"

"What does it look like?"

"The worst thing I have ever seen," Orville responds. The assembled reporters quickly scratch his answer down on their notepads and scraps of paper.

"Are you sure it's the body of Lorene Hogmire?"

O'Brien squints and grimaces as flashbulbs go off in his face.

"I don't know who else it could be," he says before being hustled away by sheriff's deputies.

As soon as O'Brien and Orville are moved away from the reporters, Sheriff James McGrath takes their place.

Anything official will come from him.

"What's next, sheriff?"

"Are you sure it's Lorene Hogmire?"

"Is Franklin Hogmire going to get the gas chamber?"

One question after another is shouted out, with no one doing McGrath the courtesy of waiting their turn.

"And where is Franklin Hogmire? Will he face charges?"

McGrath looks over his audience of reporters and photographers. He's a man comfortable in this environment who is also aware that the Hogmire story has been front-page news for a week.

In addition, McGrath, like every other elected official, knows the value of positive news coverage.

Like a robed judge banging a gavel, this badged sheriff raises his hands for quiet and to assert his authority. Once the mob of reporters calms down, he continues.

"We are confident we have recovered the body of Mrs.

Hogmire," says McGrath. "Her body was found about 300-feet from where the body of Miss Dorothy Jones was discovered.

"Mrs. Hogmire will be transported to the Moon Bay mortuary for an autopsy to determine the cause of death."

"But what about her husband?"

McGrath turns to the reporter. The sheriff sent Deputy Walter Moore and his handcuffs to San Francisco the minute McGrath learned Lorene's body had been discovered. Franklin surrendered in his room at the Harrison Hotel and is now in custody in Redwood City.

Leaving those details for a later session with reporters, McGrath only says, "Franklin Hogmire is being held for questioning. He has been taken into custody, but no charges have yet been filed."

McGrath also leaves out other information. For instance, Franklin sending his men on a wild goose chase to San Francisco by telling him his friends had seen Lorene in a dime store in "The City by The Bay."

The deputies returned empty-handed, without finding anyone who had seen Lorene in that store after her disappearance.

Franklin explained, "Oh, my mistake. My friends must have seen her with me in that store the day before she went missing."

So even though the journalists don't have that angle of the story yet -- and the sheriff hopes they never will --there's no love lost between McGrath and Franklin.

The sheriff turns away from the vultures of the press, thinking, "Now it's time to sweat this son of a bitch."

CHAPTER 63

May 3, 1946

Lorene is naked on a cold metal table inside A.P. Dutra Mortuary in Half Moon Bay.

The sun won't be up for hours. Still, Dr. Stuart Lindsay, a University of California pathologist, is finishing up his report.

"Make sure you note that we are sending specimens of Mrs. Hogmire's internal organs to Joseph Swine. He's the San Francisco city toxicologist," Dr. Lindsay tells an assistant.

"Is it too early to determine a cause of death," asks Sheriff McGrath, who eases himself off the stool that he parked himself on for the autopsy.

It's been one hell of a long day for McGrath.

Of course, he had the recovery of Lorene and the detention of Franklin to deal with. But his deputies also arrested a navy veteran, William Guernsey, and William's brother, Henry, on charges of kidnapping and raping a 21-year-old Women's Air Corp corporal, Lucille Dewey.

According to his deputy's report, the Guernsey brothers picked up Miss Dewey and a WAC private, Agnes Lababaro, before taking them on a wild Peninsula ride. Then, the brothers parked and decided to have sex with the women, whether the girls wanted it or not.

Agnes was able to escape. But Lucille was raped twice, she says, by both brothers. She says she was assaulted near Half Moon Bay and then again on a Belmont side street.

A hell of a case, but since the men had both confessed to it all,

McGrath, after doing his due diligence, turned the file over to his men to finish up the paperwork.

So for hours McGrath has been sitting on a stool with ripped plastic covering padding squeezed to the width of a dime by a variety of medical and law enforcement butts; looking over Dr. Lindsay's shoulder since late last night, watching the doctor cut into Lorene Hogmire.

"Well, there are severe gashes on both knees," says Dr. Lindsay. He glances at McGrath, then returns his attention to an assistant who's stitching up Lorene's chest.

"From the fall?"

"Maybe. But the injuries also could have been inflicted by a car's bumper."

McGrath inhales sharply. Could Franklin have run his wife off the cliff? Maybe he drove straight at Lorene, giving her the alternative of jumping to her death or being crushed under the Ford.

Damn glad, McGrath thinks, that we picked up Franklin Hogmire late last night. Not only was he needed for questioning, but Franklin was the closest living kin available to identify Lorene's body. McGrath didn't want to wait for her sisters to fly in from Texas or Oklahoma.

"Anything more?"

"Oh yes," says Dr. Lindsay. "Mrs. Hogmire suffered a concussion, but there is no fracture of the skull. In addition, she has two fractured ribs and skin burns on the right side of her body."

"So, do you think she fell or was pushed, and was dead before she hit the ground?"

Dr. Lindsay closes his notebook and looks down at Mrs. Hogmire. Two mortuary workers are in the process of moving her body off the autopsy table.

The doctor's attention returns to Sheriff McGrath.

"Like you said, it is too early to tell. The examination of the internal organs in San Francisco will tell us more."

McGrath nods, says, "Thanks," and moves to shake Dr.

Lindsay's hand. Lindsay rips off his rubber gloves to make a handshake possible.

A mortuary employee clad in black pants, a white shirt, and a skinny black tie pushes open a swinging door. That allows McGrath to escape into a hallway for a breath of air without the sickeningly sweet odor of chemicals.

He walks down the hall to the lobby and finds a phone at the front desk. McGrath picks up the receiver and dials a colleague at the San Francisco Police Department.

"McGrath here in Redwood City," he says. "Do me a favor, will ya? Impound Franklin Hogmire's Ford Coupe. It should be parked at his house. You've got the address."

McGrath hangs up and stands by himself. The mortuary is eerily quiet, even for a building whose sole function is housing the dead.

Then, he hears the squeak of small wheels that could use some oil or grease.

McGrath walks toward the sound and slowly pushes a door open, allowing him to see into a room on the right side of the hallway.

In that room, he sees the workers who'd taken Lorene's body from the autopsy, gently removing her from the metal cart that had made so much noise.

With the expertise of a couple of guys who've done this more than once, McGrath thinks, the men lay Lorene's body inside a casket.

When they back away, another man takes small, hesitant steps toward Lorene's corpse. McGrath sees two of his deputies standing near this new player but not close enough to intrude.

The man slowly sinks to his knees before the casket.

Tired as McGrath is, he hasn't slept in more than twenty-four hours, his eyes pop open.

"It's him," McGrath whispers.

While he's kneeling next to Lorene's body, Franklin's hands are clasped in front of him like a church steeple, and his lips are moving.

It takes a moment, but then McGrath mutters, "Son of a bitch didn't bat an eye when he ID'd her body last night. But now he prays?"

CHAPTER 64

May 6, 1946

This isn't the afternoon to ask anyone, "Is it hot enough for you?" There's no humor in that cliche, not today.

San Mateo County's in the midst of a heatwave. Temperatures of 88 at San Mateo and near 90 at Woodside claimed a life today.

Lou Dressler, a fifty-seven-year-old man from Burlingame, dropped dead on the San Mateo golf links. He died right in front of his wife, Constance, on the second green. The coroner's office says it looks like the Western Pipe and Steel employee fell victim to heat prostration.

The record-busting temperatures — hottest since this day in 1927 — have Franklin sweltering in the Redwood City Jail again today.

It's his fifth day being held while police continue to investigate Lorene's death.

Franklin actually requested his jail stay.

It's not that he's saying he's guilty.

No, Franklin continues to maintain his innocence in connection with Lorene's death.

He's sitting in this cell because Franklin knows something of California history and remembers what a crazed mob of regular everyday Joes did to a couple of guys accused of kidnapping and murder.

"I need to stay here until I'm cleared of all suspicion," he tells Sheriff McGrath, who is more than willing to oblige.

But Franklin isn't lonely.

Lorene's sister, Mrs. Mac Kittrell, drove in from Oklahoma City and met with Grace Johnson in San Francisco. The latter is related to Lorene and Mrs. Kittrell by marriage.

Together, the women met with Franklin.

Do they ask if he killed Lorene? No. Instead, the women want to talk about funeral arrangements for Lorene.

That, however, isn't the only item on the itinerary of Grace and Mrs. Kittrell. They're also planning to take in the double feature at the Manor Theater tomorrow night.

Anything to take their minds of this tragedy.

"Couple of great pictures," says Grace. "'Don Juan Quilligan with Joan Blondell and William Bendix. And then, they're showing a new George Raft movie, 'Nob Hill.'

"Don't know what it's about, but it is some kind of a musical. And get this, the theater is giving away free ovenware at the door."

So Mrs. Kittrell phones home to Mac to say she'll be staying an extra day. Maybe two.

But there is more than exploring Redwood City's nightlife on her mind. Same with Grace.

Mrs. Kittrell and Grace spent more than an hour talking to Chief Deputy Walter Moore and Deputy Jack O'Brien before chatting with Franklin.

"Franklin called me two days after Lorene went missing," Mrs. Kittrell tells the officers.

"What was on his mind?" Chief Deputy Moore says after passing Mrs. Kittrell a handkerchief to wipe tears from her eyes.

She looks at Moore, sniffs, and says, "Franklin told me that he was afraid Lorene had been murdered."

Moore and O'Brien look at each other, then after a few more questions and answers, dismiss the ladies.

"What do you think?" O'Brien says. "It is looking more and more like she was murdered. At least that's what I think."

"It's still too soon to say. We aren't going to get the toxicology report from Joe Swine in San Francisco until Saturday, at least. That's another five days before we find out if there was any organ damage."

"True, but we followed her trail pretty well. We know she either fell or was shoved off an observation platform at the edge of the cliff."

"I'll give you that one:"

"And the platform is about fifty feet south of where we found her body. On top of that, it looks like she tumbled right down a dry gully. You couldn't miss the trail. We found two sticks of chewing gum, her coin purse, two dollars in change, a key to the Hogmire's Ford, a button from her slacks, and a bandana."

"Christ, she must have lost it all while she was falling."

"Yeah. There were bloodstains about seventy-five feet from where me and Orville found the body."

Moore says, "It looks like that's where she broke her fall, where the blood was. But then she must have squirmed around or tried to walk and fell again, down those last seventy-five feet."

Moore sips from the lukewarm coffee in his cup.

"You know Lindsay says she could have been alive for an hour, maybe more after she finally stopped falling," he adds.

O'Brien takes a swig of his own lukewarm coffee. "Jesus. Could she have really slipped and fallen all that way? You don't think she was shoved?"

Moore leans back in his chair.

"What about those state highway workers?"

O'Brien flips open his notepad. "You mean George Pimentel and Thomas Fahey?"

"Yeah. Didn't those guys find the Hogmire's coupe?"

"Sure did," says O'Brien. "They spotted it at eight in the morning, the day Lorene disappeared. And they said it was empty. Nobody in sight."

"Until —"

"Right. Until George and Thomas looked over a cliff and saw Hogmire working in a gully about one-hundred feet south of that platform Lorene fell from."

"But Hogmire tells us he went to work at around 8:30 or 9 o'clock."

"Said he kissed Lorene goodbye and then lowered himself down to start searching for Thora Chamberlain's body."

"So, a half-hour, maybe a full hour after those state highway guys say the Hogmire's Ford was empty, Franklin says he was kissing Lorene goodbye."

"And the day after his wife vanishes, Hogmire says he was searching for her about fifty feet from where we discovered that sandal."

"And about two-hundred feet from where you found Lorene's body."

O'Brien closes his notepad with a flourish

"So, what do you think?"

Moore crosses his arms over his chest.

He says, "I think it's time we talk to Frank Marlowe, the chief inspector in the DA's office, about setting up a lie detector test for our friend, Franklin Hogmire."

CHAPTER 65

May 8, 1946

A thin rubber strap connects his left arm to the lie detector machine. And, Franklin tells the bow-tie-wearing polygraph operator everything he'd already told Sheriff McGrath many times over.

"Like I said before, Lorene and I went up on Devil's Slide to look for Thora Chamberlain's body. I kissed my wife goodbye, went down to search around, came back up for lunch, and she was gone."

His story doesn't change during the thirty minutes Franklin spends locked in a tiny room. Just him, the lie detector, and its human operator who can't weigh 120 pounds soaking wet.

And even though he's sweating like a man facing his own execution — which he might be — the little mechanical arm reacting to his every word scratches out a straight line of honesty.

After another half-hour talking to the polygraph operator who has packed up his equipment, Sheriff McGrath walks into a room where Deputy Sheriff Jack O'Brien and Chief Deputy Walter Moore are waiting for him.

"Well, good news for Hogmire," McGrath says. "He sailed through the polygraph. Didn't tell a single lie."

The sturdy shoulders of O'Brien and Moore sag.

"And on top of that," says McGrath, "the preliminary toxicology report came back from San Francisco this morning."

He makes a show of removing Joseph Swine's three-page

memo from its folder.

"According to this, boys, our Mrs. Hogmire was loaded, blotto, when she took her dive off the cliff. The report here says there's no doubt that she was under the influence of alcohol."

"So John Barleycorn killed Lorene Hogmire," says Moore.

"Looks like it," McGrath replies. "District Attorney Ferrell says he wants me to check out a few more angles, but I don't think there's any doubt that Franklin Hogmire is going to be a free man by supper time."

A few hours later, Franklin's packing the few possessions he brought into the San Mateo County Jail.

"A small army of reporters is out there waiting for you," says a guard. "Want us to sneak you out the back way?"

Franklin's worked up something close to a friendship with the men guarding him, and he appreciates the offer.

"That's not a bad idea, thanks."

As Franklin grabs his knapsack to leave, District Attorney Gilbert Ferrell walks into his cell.

Franklin freezes, and his face goes white. What could have gone wrong, now?

"Don't worry," Ferrell says, "you're a free man, almost."

"Almost?"

"Yeah, don't get yourself lost. San Mateo County will need you again if we prosecute McMonigle for the murder of that woman whose body you found at Devil's Slide."

Franklin's face goes rock hard. The last place he wants to settle down in is San Mateo County or even California. His thumb is already itching to find a ride as soon as he finds his way to a highway.

Any road that leads away from Devil's Slide and the Pacific Ocean, will be good enough for Franklin.

Sensing Franklin's desire to leave town, Ferrell says, "Don't make us come looking for you."

Franklin tips his hat to Ferrell and grabs his pack. He ambles to the front door. Feels like talking to reporters all of a sudden.

Once outside, the questions are fired at him like the .50-caliber machine gun he lived with during the war.

A young man with a pencil and notepad at the ready shouts, "Are you innocent?"

"What happened to your wife, Lorene?" A portly older man shouts this question even though he looks like he'd rather be at the police station eating doughnuts with his cop buddies.

From the lone female scribe in the pack, Franklin hears, "Were the two of you having marriage problems?"

Franklin smiles slowly and raises his hands for quiet.

"I only have a couple of things to say, fellas, and ma'am. To begin with, answering your question, young lady, if we, Lorene and me, were having marriage problems I was the last to know.

"I will admit Lorene told a waitress at the cafe where she worked that she made a mistake in divorcing Ballard and marrying me. But I only learned about that recently."

"Are you serious?"

Franklin shrugs his shoulders. "Lorene never mentioned it to me."

"But what about you," yells another reporter, "are you innocent?"

Franklin smiles again and adjusts his hat. It's obvious he's ready to scram.

As he walks down the concrete steps leading Franklin to the next chapter of his life, the sea of reporters parts.

Looking over his shoulder, Franklin stops.

"I knew all along I was innocent, but I am glad the police are helping me to clear me through the lie detector."

He bounces down the remaining steps with a jaunty smile on his face. Franklin's mood, however, soon changes.

As stone-cold serious now as he was in battle, he hails a taxi.

Whether Franklin intends to follow Ferrell's admonition to stay in California is yet to be seen. However, before this humble junk dealer even gets close to the state line, he has one more stop to make.

After getting a couple of drinks, a fresh pack of Lucky Strikes, some supper, and a change of clothes, Franklin will attend Lorene's funeral in Half Moon Bay.

CHAPTER 66

March 14, 1947

San Quentin's warden, Clinton Duffy, thought he'd seen it all until this morning. He's just finished reading a proposal from someone who sounds like a mad scientist.

"This is from a guy named Cornish," says Duffy. He waves several pages of stationery in the air. "He wants to experiment on one of our inmates, Thomas McMonigle, and see if he can bring him back from the dead after he's executed in the gas chamber.

"And guess what? McMonigle wants him to try."

"Well, who wouldn't want to at least try," says the aide sitting on the other side of Duffy's desk. "After all, what's McMonigle got to lose?"

Duffy laughs and says, "Cornish says here in his proposal that McMonigle; he's the guy that killed that girl, Thora Chamberlain, right?"

The aide nods his agreement.

"Anyway, Cornish says here that McMonigle, like he's some kind of saint or something, is offering his body for the experiment in the interests of humanity.

"'He wants me to bring him back to life,' Cornish writes in this letter, 'in the interests of the thousands who die of shock, asphyxiation, and drowning.'"

"Have you ever heard of this guy, Cornish?"

"I hadn't until his request came in, but he is the real deal," says the aide.

"You're telling me he can really bring people back from the dead?"

"Well, not yet, but he's trying."

Duffy's second-in-command opens a folder, puts on a pair of wire-rimmed glasses, and begins reading aloud from the pages in front of him.

"Dr. Robert Cornish, born in 1903, was a child prodigy. He graduated from the University of California in Berkley with honors when he was eighteen and then got his doctorate four years later.

"Cornish has been trying for more than a dozen years to bring people back from the dead. He built a teeterboard or see-saw device. He puts the recently departed on the board. After that, Cornish plugs them into a machine. The device pumps a mix of epinephrine and anticoagulants into the dead person's bloodstream.

"Then Cornish rocks the teeter-totter device up and down to get the blood flowing again in the dead person."

"Oh, for Christ's sake."

The aide pauses to smile and take a sip of water. Then, he continues.

"Cornish spent most of 1933 trying to resurrect dead people who had succumbed to heart attacks, drowning, and electrocution.

"So far, he has not brought any humans back from the dead. However, two dogs — Lazarus IV and V — were clinically put to death and then brought back to life in 1934 and 1935."

"Dogs? Good Lord. How'd they do?"

"Not well, according to what I've read.

"But, a couple of humans have volunteered to be brought back to life. One was a prisoner scheduled to be hanged; the other was a man in his late seventies who figured he'd had a good life and wanted to help science.

"Cornish considered the first patient but wound up rejecting him. He needs someone who has died without physical injury. It seems like getting your windpipe crushed in a hangman's noose means you'd need more than a magic fluid and a teeter-totter to come back to life.

"The second guy was told 'thanks but no thanks,' because Cornish would have had to kill him first, which would have made our young scientist a murderer.

"Back in 1933 and '34, Cornish went to the governors of Arizona, Colorado, and Nevada, asking if they'd let him try to revive prisoners who'd been executed in the states' gas chambers."

"I can hardly wait to hear what they had to say."

The aide sips more water before continuing.

He shuffles the pages.

"Warden Penrose of the Nevada state penitentiary said Cornish was welcome to try to resurrect the dead in his gas chamber. But Penrose said the doctor would be risking his life."

"How so?"

"Cornish says he has to hook up the dead person to his machine in just a few minutes after the convict dies.

"Penrose said it takes ten minutes to remove the lethal gas from the gas chamber. So Cornish could die while retrieving the dead body."

"But Dr. Cornish says he understands the dangers associated with San Quentin's gas chamber. That's why he plans to don a gas mask before entering the room of death a few minutes after Thomas is pronounced dead.

"'I'll bring the body out of the execution chamber and immediately begin bringing Thomas McMonigle back to life within the walls of the prison.'"

Duffy's back stiffens. This is the last thing he needs at San Quentin.

The aide sees his boss is even more tense than usual, but continues.

"The scientist also says the attempted revivification would follow human blood pumping back into Thomas's arteries, saturated with oxygen.

"'I'll know within five minutes if the heart is going to begin pumping blood again,' says Cornish. 'And within thirty minutes, I should know if a man can be brought back to life after inhaling a lethal dose of cyanide gas.'"

The aide pauses to let that sink in.

He continues, "Even with all of that, Penrose also says he thinks there could be a legal problem if Cornish's plan works.

"You see, Nevada's death penalty law stipulates that the convicted killer 'remain in prison until dead.'

"So, as Penrose sees it, anyone brought back to life would have to immediately go back into the gas chamber and be executed a second time."

Duffy drums his fingers on the wooden desk.

"What about the others?"

"Arizona Gov. B.B. Moeur rejected Cornish's proposal outright, not even dignifying it with much of an official statement.

"However, the warden at Sing Sing Prison in upstate New York didn't mince words. Lewis E. Lawes called Cornish's proposal 'absolutely ridiculous.'"

"I'd have to agree with that," says Duffy.

"But get this. Colorado Governor Ed C. Johnson was the outlier in this debate. Johnson said he would at least talk to Cornish about the idea since Colorado already offered to free two convicts who were willing to undergo tuberculosis test experiments."

"What happened there?"

"Guess it didn't pan out.

"Then McMonigle hears about Cornish, writes to him, and here we are."

"No, I'd have to say, 'here we ain't,'" says Duffy. "You call Cornish, and tell McMonigle, that there's no way some mad scientist is going to set up shop in San Quentin.

"It's as simple as this. Either the next of kin will claim McMonigle's body, or he will be buried in the prison cemetery.

"Nobody is going to bring this killer back to life."

CHAPTER 67

March 15, 1947

In Moscow today, the Allies are still trying to figure out how to put the world back together.

French diplomats are floating a unique idea: move Germans out of Germany to lower their potential to launch a counter-attack.

Interesting.

However, the plan does present a perplexing question: What should be done with millions of Germans force-marched out of their homeland?

Surprisingly, the French diplomats say they'd be welcomed in France.

Rebuilding the world after years of war is not going smoothly.

In Washington D.C., Sen. Robert A. Taft wants to know what top U.S. military brass think of speculation in Europe that Russia might declare war on the United States.

Some say World War Three is possible if President Truman gives financial and military aid to Greece and Turkey.

Sen. Taft worries Moscow will unleash its military if the U.S. delivers the aid.

"Just as we might be prompted to go to war," Taft says, "if Russia tried to force a Communist government on Cuba."

On the other side of the world, rumors are rampant across the Pacific in Tokyo this week about America getting ready to launch another World War.

So, if there is one constant in the rumors, everybody's talking about the United States and Russia going to war. The question is no longer "if." The only unanswered query on the streets of Tokyo is "when and where."

United Press reports that many Japanese are convinced the third World War is not only imminent but will be launched on the streets of Tokyo because of Japan's proximity to the Soviet Union.

The only land border between Japan and the Soviet Union is a line drawn down the middle of the island of Sakhalin. But that was erased when the Soviet Army captured the island in 1945.

Since then, the nations have only been separated by a 194.3 km maritime boundary.

So, there's nothing but water keeping the Soviets from Japanese soil.

But in his Death Row cell, all Thomas can think about is being turned down by a teenage girl again. He feels rejected and dejected.

Not only was his offer to donate his body to science dismissed by Warden Duffy yesterday, but now he's learned a fifteen-year-old girl has turned thumbs down to Thomas's offer to help her see again.

"This isn't right," Thomas remarked to a fellow Death Row inmate months ago. "A teenage girl is going blind, and her school in L.A. says she can't bring her seeing-eye dog into class."

"Going blind?" An inmate Thomas has never seen — killers are kept apart in the "Q" — shouts his question from down the way.

"Yeah," answers Thomas. "Says here in the paper that Patsy Ruth Fergus — the blind girl — has clear corneas, but her retina has not fully developed."

"So she's blind? What are you going to do about it?"

Thomas folds the paper and sets it down.

"I'm going to give her my eyes," he says.

"Your eyes?"

"Sure. Won't need them where I am going. The doctors, I'll bet, could transplant them right into her head. It'd be as simple as screwing in a new light bulb."

Thomas's attorney helped him track down Patsy's address and sent a letter to her parents with the offer.

This time, however, neither state law nor Warden Duffy got in the way.

Thomas reads her letter twice to make sure he's not mistaken. But, there's no room for doubt.

Patsy tells Thomas to keep his eyes to himself. And, she explains, it's nothing personal.

"It would be wonderful to see again," Patsy says, "but I don't like the idea of seeing through a dead person's eyes."

CHAPTER 68

May 26, 1947

Thomas McMonigle is not a man who readily accepts defeat, and why would he? After all, Thomas is fighting for his life.

Today, he's scheduled to appear before Federal Judge Michael Roche in San Francisco for a hearing on a legal brief that Thomas himself wrote.

The thesis of his brief, already rejected by the Supreme Court of California, is that the FBI used intimidation and violence to win Thomas's confession and conviction for Thora's murder.

Unrelated to today's hearing, which most of the reporters and legal minds following the case expect to be quickly tossed into Judge Roche's bin, Thomas has a medical appointment tomorrow.

Specifically, Thomas wants an eye exam. Despite his offer to Patsy Ruth Fergus, Thomas says he is now absolutely sure that he is going blind.

What does Warden Clinton Duffy think of that?

The warden told a reporter from the San Francisco Examiner it's "just another of McMonigle's stories."

CHAPTER 69

June 17, 1947

Franklin's working on a farm in Oklahoma today. Never one to willingly follow the instructions of those in authority, he didn't spend more than a few days of the past year in the county of San Mateo or even the state of California.

But he satisfied the county law enforcement community by promising to keep in touch.

So far, Franklin's kept that promise. Maybe he'll soon be sorry that he was so compliant.

He doesn't know it this morning, but Franklin's about to get a phone call tomorrow from his law enforcement buddies in San Mateo County.

Here's why:

Flanked by San Quentin Prison Warden Clinton Duffy and Prison Officer Tom Cheatham, while Franklin's happily toiling in a field, Thomas walks out of the California Supreme Court a happy man.

Sure. Thomas's hands are cuffed in front of him. And, on one side is Cheatham, on the other is Duffy.

So, he's hardly a free man. One more thing that might depress a lesser man. The eye doctor who examined Thomas told the confessed murderer that he is not going blind.

So, as Clinton Duffy speculated, Thomas's concern about his vision resulted from either hypochondria or Thomas's desire to avoid the gas chamber.

Or perhaps it was just another of his stories.

Either way, Thomas has also learned Dr. Cornish will not be allowed to bring him back from the dead.

When it rains, it pours, right?

But Thomas's jaunty smile is back.

Hell's bells. Who wouldn't be smiling?

He's wearing a snazzy suit, and for the first time in more than a year, Thomas is outside the walls of San Quentin's Death Row.

That's not the only reason for his happiness.

He's going to be alive three months longer than the state of California had planned, up until a few hours ago.

Thomas just won a ninety-day stay of his death penalty. And if things keep going his way, he just might cheat death.

Earlier today, wearing a grey suit, white shirt, and a patterned tie, Thomas, once his handcuffs are removed, arguing as his own attorney, looks up at the justices sitting high above him and calmly presents his petition for a writ of habeas corpus.

Cracking the law books available to him in prison, Thomas knows the Latin phrase means "let you have the body."

"It's a way to report an unlawful detention or illegal confinement," Thomas reads aloud to one of his buddies, lips moving as his finger following the sentence in front of him.

That is just what Thomas is doing today.

He accuses the FBI of detaining him "seven days incommunicado." Thomas also tells the justices that the federal agents beat him.

In addition, Thomas says that he had to tolerate "constant gunfire directly outside the courtroom during his trial."

After hearing Thomas's arguments and going through his paperwork, the supreme court named Superior Judge Samuel F. Finley of Del Norte County to serve as a special referee in the case.

It will be Finley's job to retrace Thomas's entire trial.

Finley will re-read the case transcript, along with talking to all of the attorneys and officials involved. Along with that, Finley will summon witnesses who might be able to shed new light on testimony and evidence presented during Thomas's trial.

"I'm going to call new witnesses to the stand," Thomas tells his San Quentin buddies after writing up his legal brief. "I've got a list of sixty-five names."

Reading the sheet Thomas handed him, a literate inmate looks up in amazement.

"You actually think you're going to get J. Edgar Hoover, and Eleanor Roosevelt, to testify?"

One of the guards who overhears the conversation looks over the inmate's shoulder then up at Thomas.

"McMonigle," the guard says, "you are crazy like a fox."

CHAPTER 70

June 18, 1947

A 20-year-old on probation from the San Mateo County courts is sitting in the county jail today after confessing to pulling off twenty-two armed robberies in just two months in San Francisco.

Described by the San Mateo Times as a "sleepy-looking six-footer," William Orville McNamara was convicted last year of leading a gang that stole more than three hundred blank checks from a paint shop. They used the checks to fleece $10,000 from Bay Area merchants.

He got off with a probationary slap on the wrist. But guess what? Here William is today, back behind bars.

Obviously, McNamara's criminal ways got the better of him, and he took off on a crime spree. There's no way any judge is going to let William run free again. He'll be spending more than a few years, doing hard time, behind bars now.

Another bad guy off the streets.

On an average day, that would give San Mateo County Deputy Sheriff Walter Moore plenty of reason to celebrate.

But not today.

Close to a year after Moore figured he could put the case and file of one, Thomas Henry McMonigle, out of his mind and off his desk; he gets slapped in the face with it again.

Moore and his fellow deputies couldn't be more enraged, and they are not going to take this lying down.

Now, it's not like they haven't gone down this road before.

In December, the state supreme court heard a request for Thomas's automatic appeal, a legal move that accompanies all death sentences. The justices affirmed his conviction and, in February of this year, the appeal was denied.

In March, Thomas filed another appeal which was rejected. Then, his new lawyer from San Francisco filed a federal appeal on Thomas's behalf, which was also nixed.

Thomas is set to die on June 20, in just a couple of days. So, this latest move is probably, also, his last hope.

The day after receiving the news that the Supreme Court was giving Thomas another ninety days to live, along with reopening the murder of Thora Chamberlain, Moore declares that if Thomas wins this case, he will be quickly prosecuted for the murder of Dorothy Rose Jones.

But before Moore vents his outrage to a room of reporters, he places a phone call to a farm in Oklahoma and rousts Franklin Hogmire out of the junk man's deep sleep.

"You're going to be our star witness," Moore tells Franklin after bringing the groggy widower up to date on the latest in the Thomas McMonigle saga.

Getting only a blurry mumble as a reply, Moore goes into greater detail.

"You found the Negro woman's body," explains Moore. "And that is our key piece of evidence."

"But I thought you said the little jerk confessed to the cops in San Francisco?"

"Yeah, he did. But McMonigle could skate on the Thora Chamberlain murder because we couldn't produce her body. The lawyers call it, not having 'corpus delecti.'"

"What?"

"It's Latin. 'The Body of the Crime.' Didn't you go to school?"

"So, what's that mean to me?"

"It means you are going to have to get your ass back here to San Mateo."

"Oh, for Christ's sake.'

"Hey, don't blaspheme on me. You stumbling upon the body of Dorothy Rose Jones means everything to this case and putting McMonigle where he belongs, which is in the gas chamber."

A few hours later, with Franklin's safe passage to the county of San Mateo all but assured, Moore is standing in that room full of journalists.

They all know that Moore and the District Attorney's Office got sucker-punched by the Supreme Court. And some of the scribes are smirking.

"You're afraid McMonigle is going to go free," shouts a reporter with the loudest voice in the room.

The pulp journalist's statement is followed by many more of the same vein.

Moore is not about to be intimidated.

"McMonigle is going to the gas chamber," Moore says. "If the Supreme Court reverses his conviction for killing Thora Chamberlain, we will prosecute him for the murder of Dorothy Rose Jones.

"San Francisco police have a signed confession from McMonigle in which he admits killing the Negro woman and then throwing her body off a cliff into the Pacific Ocean."

Knowing he has a slightly more educated audience than he had on the phone earlier, he goes for the Latin.

"No corpus delecti was established in the case of the schoolgirl," Moore says. "But a body was found and established as the second victim of McMonigle's murderous frenzy.

"I promise you, Thomas Henry McMonigle will not cheat death."

CHAPTER 71

February 19, 1948

Burlingame Police Captain John Hartnett, Chief Deputy Sheriff Walter Moore, and Deputy District Attorney Henry Davis can't believe the documents laid out in front of them.

Nor can they believe where they are at 9 p.m. on this cold February night.

In front of them, a map and adjacent paperwork, all held down by four rocks to keep them from blowing away in the cold wind that has the men shivering.

The men were called to an emergency conference at the Blair Company construction yard this evening. The call came from Thomas's attorney, James Montgomery, who replaced the Death Row inmate's legal aid team.

"I have important information to present from my client," Montgomery said in his phone calls. "You are going to want to see what I have because it could lead you to find the body of Thora Chamberlain."

When Hartnett expresses his skepticism, "haven't we see enough from McMonigle," Montgomery assures the police captain the meeting will not be a waste of time.

"This is an opportunity to ease the grief of this girl's family," says Montgomery. "In addition, you need to know that copies of this information are in the hands of several reporters."

What choice do Hartnett and the others have?

The three law enforcers appear as requested by Montgomery to see the map that the attorney says could end the Thora

Chamberlain saga once and for all.

If nothing else, the map could amount to Thomas's jailhouse confession.

He doesn't have long.

The Supreme Court of California rejected Thomas's writ of habeas corpus petition in December. The justices also rebuked him for wasting the time of state and federal courts.

Maybe they had a point.

Thomas beseeched California's Supreme Court with writ petitions three times since he was convicted of murdering Thora, and each time, he lost.

The last time, Superior Court Judge Samuel F. Finley was appointed as a special referee to hear Thomas's allegations and charges of judicial error. Judge Finley ruled there was no basis for Thomas's writ petition.

A Supreme Court decision released on December 30 of last year supported Finley's decision.

The Court also accused Thomas of making: "repeated attempts" to obtain writs of habeas corpus and using "false allegations" to "obtain unwarranted delays in the execution of the sentence imposed."

Of course, that sentence is death.

Gov. Earl Warren granted Thomas a reprieve until tomorrow, February 20, to allow the convicted child-killer one last chance. But with the December Supreme Court decision, Thomas can see the finish line.

Barring some unforeseen revelation, Thomas is going to die tomorrow.

The imminent departure of Mr. McMonigle is on the minds of everyone in attorney Montgomery's office this evening as he unrolls the map Thomas spent several days drawing.

"As you can see," says Montgomery, "you'll find the body of Miss Chamberlain buried in a rectangular area about 500 feet north of the Blair Company construction yard and about a hundred feet south from a building that has since been torn down on the edge of the corporation's yard."

Montgomery looks each man in the eye before continuing.

"Thomas McMonigle swears that he put Miss Chamberlain's body in a wooden packing crate that he got from his home in San Mateo.

"Once the girl was placed in the crate, my client says he buried her three feet below the surface."

While the others are mulling over the map, Montgomery continues.

"You'll note that this area has not been dug over before. Here's another important point," the attorney says as he jabs the map with his finger for emphasis. "It's about 200 to 300 feet north of where the FBI found the girl's books and a pair of shoes."

While the others lean over the map, Hartnett throws his hands into the air.

He's sick to death of jumping through hoops set up by Thomas, and Hartnett makes no attempt to hide his new level of disgust with the murderer of a teenage girl.

Still, he has to admit Montgomery is correct.

No one on the search team ever turned a shovel of dirt in this area. At the time Thomas says he buried Thora's body at this site, it was nothing more than a garbage dump connected to the Blair construction yard.

Since then, the land's been sold to Harry Lee Plumbing.

"How can we go out there and dig tonight?" Hartnett says. "Since Lee bought the land, it's been filled with six or more feet of earth and rock topping.

"In addition, Harry Lee constructed a building with a cement floor over part of the area where McMonigle says he buried the girl.

"That means we'd have to dig nine or more feet deep in a 200-square-foot area.

"It's an impossible task."

"Hartnett's correct," says Chief Deputy Sheriff Moore. "And we don't even know where to start. The exact spot might be right under the building with the cement floor."

"If we are to believe this map and McMonigle's statements, it means he was doing nothing but giving us the runaround when he said he buried Thora's body south of this spot," says Deputy D.A. Davis.

"Why the hell should we believe him now?"

Shivering, the others nod their agreement.

But one other guest invited by Montgomery believes the word of Thomas McMonigle.

None other than Thomas's ex-wife, Ena, is standing with the men. She seems almost gleeful, examining the map.

"I have a feeling the girl is buried right here," the former Mrs. McMonigle says.

Hartnett and the others, ready to get into their cars and turn the heaters on high, are a chorus of cynics.

"And just where did he get the packing crate from," says one of the lawmen.

Ena thinks for a moment before saying, "Oh, that. I just remembered we had two packing crates at the house. Thomas came home with them when he worked for a storage company before getting a job at Blair's.

"And you know what?" Ena rests a finger on the side of her face. "It seems to me like one of those packing crates is missing.

"Sorry. I do wish I'd thought of that sooner."

All of the men, except Montgomery, shake their heads and walk to their cars.

Despite what Ena might believe, no one will be putting a shovel into this ground before Thomas goes to the gas chamber tomorrow.

As Hartnett, Moore, and Davis leave, Montgomery places a hand on Ena's elbow to hold her back.

"Will you be at San Quentin tomorrow to claim Thomas's body?"

Ena looks at him and chuckles.

"Oh dear God, no."

CHAPTER 72

February 20, 1948

A heavy morning fog lifts, replaced with bright sunshine.
It's 10 a.m. at San Quentin.
Thomas's life will be over in less than half an hour.
Two years and two days after his conviction, Thomas will be strapped into a chair in San Quentin's gas chamber this morning, a lever pulled, and a sackful of poison tablets will be released, ending his life.
Legal appeals exhausted, the map to what Thomas claims is Thora's final resting place ignored, he's walking into the execution chamber, white-faced and glassy-eyed, as if he can't believe this is happening.
Thomas held out hope that Gov. Earl Warren would intervene even as he sat down to a meager breakfast a few hours ago that included ham, eggs, and a glass of fruit juice.
But as it became apparent no one was going to save Thomas from the gas chamber, he could only nibble at the toast and pick at his ham and eggs.
Before this death march began, three prison psychiatrists spent time with Thomas to ensure he was not insane and understood what would happen this morning.
The doctors pronounce Thomas sane yet note that he is "agitated" and "not reconciled to the death sentence because he says the courts have no corpus delicti."
Thomas received holy communion from Father Daniel McAlister, the Catholic chaplain at San Quentin last night. Now,

Father McAlister walks by Thomas's side, praying for God's mercy.

Thomas's customary swagger is gone. Barefoot. Wearing only blue jeans and a white shirt. Eyes glassy but also beet red, it's obvious he hasn't slept a wink in the last twenty-four hours of his life.

Rather than closing his eyes, Thomas spent the night smoking cigars with his guards and joking with them about the cheap smokes. Before him sat the remains of a fried chicken dinner that he hardly touched.

Thomas had less appetite last night than he had this morning.

As he leaves his cell for the last time, Thomas hands Warden Clinton Duffy a piece of paper folded in half. The warden glances at it and turns back to Thomas.

"Ready to go," says Duffy, who called Gov. Warren's office less than an hour ago to make sure there'd be no change in the execution plans.

Then, Warden Duffy, Thomas, and Father McAlister begin that final walk, the walk of a dead man.

At one point, Father McAlister grasps Thomas's hand as the dead man walking begins stumbling like a drunken man.

However, as Thomas gets closer to the gas chamber, his old personality returns. A group of physicians stops him so they can bind a stethoscope to his chest.

"Don't strap it too tight," Thomas chuckles.

Seventy-two witnesses, jam against a railing keeping them from the glass windows of the steel chamber of death, as Thomas is led into the execution chamber. All men. No women. That's the state law. Females are forbidden from witnessing executions. The men who write the laws in Sacramento probably thought it was for their own good.

Those in attendance are mainly newspapermen, San Mateo County sheriff's deputies, and San Mateo police officers. While most sit silently, there are triumphant smiles and even jokes from the law enforcement officers.

They got their man.

Now, they'll watch Thomas die.

Attending physicians will use that stethoscope taped to Thomas's chest and connected to a rubber tube to determine the exact moment of his death.

Thomas, who's become known nationwide for his carefree, cavalier attitude, isn't smiling nor smirking anymore.

Instead, he keeps his head bowed, never glancing at those who will see him inhale a cloud of poison. Does he even notice the gas chamber's steel walls are painted apple-green?

He grimaces. Sobs. And sits in one of two wooden chairs in the gas chamber.

Damn.

It's the wrong chair.

The last mistake Thomas McMonigle will ever make on this earth, right?

A muscular guard standing behind Thomas lifts the condemned man and sets him down in the proper chair.

Thomas understands how to make these last moments of his life as pain-free as possible.

Thomas sits with shoulders erect, but his head is still down, so he'll be able to take his final breaths and quickly inhale the noxious fumes coming from beneath him that will bring an end to his life.

Once he's settled, outside Thomas's death chamber, a guard pushes a lever, releasing a pound of cyanide pellets from a cheesecloth sack.

At 10:02:30 a.m., Thomas looks up briefly and opens his eyes as he listens to the rumble of those pellets falling into a well of sulphuric acid and distilled water beneath his chair.

Next, Thomas and his final audience see a cloud of fumes rising from the mixture.

No laughs, smiles, or jokes now. The seventy-two watching Thomas's last moments hush.

Thomas, at first, holds his breath. Then, a moment later, almost eagerly, he takes a long, deep breath. His lungs fill with cyanide gas. Thomas looks up to the ceiling for a few seconds before his head falls.

Thomas's nostrils twice, and his shoulders shake. Although Thomas's hands are not clenched in fists, his right thumb looks like it's biting into the finger next to it.

Four minutes pass.

Thomas raises his head once more, then begins coughing violently.

As the clock ticks off three more seconds, Thomas begins to breathe normally. He takes several breaths before his head, again, slumps forward.

Shortly after 10:14 a.m., Thomas's head shakes, almost, it seems, involuntarily.

Sixty seconds later, the prison doctor, hearing a final heartbeat through that stethoscope lashed to his chest, declares Thomas is no longer of this earth.

Thomas Henry McMonigle is dead.

CHAPTER 73

The reporters and cops who chronicled and cheered Thomas's death are on their way home from San Quentin.

While they're driving to file their stories and have dinner with their loved ones, Father McAlister waits outside the gas chamber. He's standing alone, behind two panes of glass, in the room where the seventy-two watched Thomas die.

It's a long wait. The patience of a religious man is well needed.

More than an hour later, Thomas's body is still strapped to the wooden chair where the convicted killer was put to death. A special crew continues "scrubbing" the metal enclosure to ensure none of the deadly cyanide fumes remain.

Finally, at 11:30, Thomas's body is released to Father McAlister. He's claiming the corpse.

What else is he going to do?

Ena, who visited Thomas two days ago, made it clear again that she doesn't want anything to do with her ex-husband's body. And she told him so.

"I'd rather just start my life all over again," Ena tells Thomas. "I have to do that for our little girl."

While Father McAlister waits, Warden Duffy opens the note passed to him by Thomas and begins reading:

"I, Thomas Henry McMonigle, in this last testimony to the people, declare that I did not shoot Thora Chamberlain and I did not throw her body over a cliff.

"I never made any confession that I shot Thora Chamberlain in Santa Cruz County."

Duffy re-folds the paper and wonders, "did we convict the wrong man?"

He also considers whether he should just throw the note away or release it to the newspapers.

It doesn't take long for the warden of San Quentin to make up his mind.

Duffy tells his aide, "We got the right man. McMonigle might say he didn't shoot Thora Chamberlain and toss her body off a cliff. But he never says that he did not kill the girl.

"After all the stories McMonigle crafted about what happened, how are we going to believe this one?"

With that, Duffy crumbles the note and tosses it to his aide for disposal. The paper that held Thomas Henry McMonigle's last words will soon be ashes.

During the middle of the afternoon, Father McAlister, with Thomas's corpse, goes next to a cemetery near San Rafael. It's a sad, lonely journey, the purpose of which is to lay Thomas to rest in a charity plot.

The Father performs a service for one.

He walks away, a priest with his Bible, while the gravediggers are tapping down the dirt over Thomas's cheap wooden casket.

Meanwhile, reporters call Thora Chamberlain's parents.

The response never varies. Frank and Lois reject every journalistic inquiry with a simple "no comment."

Outside her home, newspaper and radio reporters, however, do find Ena is willing to talk.

One of the journalists asks if Ena believes her ex-husband murdered Thora Chamberlain.

Ena sighs as she considers her answer.

"What's the point?" Ena says. "He confessed, and there is nothing else to be done."

Before another question can be asked, Ena turns to leave. She's holding the hand of a little girl, her and Thomas's daughter, born just a few days before Thora disappeared.

Ena stops, looks back over her shoulder, and says, "Perhaps it will all be for the best."

BIBLIOGRAPHY

"Doctor Seeks To Revive Lethal Gas Cell Victims," Honolulu Advertiser, published 16 October 1934

"Youth, Aged man Offer to Die For Berkeley Scientist in His Experiment to Resurrect Dead," Santa Rosa Republican, published 17 October 1934.

"Marie Wallman in Song Recital," Oakland Tribune, 22 May 1935.

"Jubilee Boys Draw Dialers To Station KLX," Oakland Tribune, published 7 May 1936.

"Garden. Club Exhibit Set in Berkeley," Oakland Tribune, published 29 October 1937.

"Hope of Finding Lost Girl Grows," Star-Tribune, published 7 November 1945.

"Cranks Harass Tum Suden Kin," San Francisco Examiner, published 9 November 1945.

"Thora Hunted in Long Beach on New Tip," San Francisco Examiner, published 9 November 1945.

"National Health Insurance System Proposed by Truman," Press Democrat, published 20 November 1945.

"Box Office Reporter," Campbell Press, published 22 November 1945.

"S.M. Man Confesses Killing Girl," San Mateo Times, published 15 December 1945.

"Mountain View Schoolgirl's Body in Ocean," San Francisco Examiner, published 16 December 1945.

"16 S.M. Girls Signed Plea for McMonigle," San Mateo Times, published 17 December 1945.

"O'Brien Praised for Capture of M'Monigle," San Mateo Times, published 17 December 1945.

"3 Counties May Lay Claim to McMonigle," San Mateo Times, published 17 December 1945.

"UNO Demands Title to Land in Winning City; Will Visit U.S. Sites," San Mateo Times, published 17 December 1945.

"Hold Killer Suspect in San Quentin," Madera Tribune, published 17 December 1945.

"M'Monigle Indicted in San Jose as Kidnapper," San Francisco Examiner, published 19 December 1945.

"More Drastic Charge Awaits Finding of Body," San Francisco Examiner, 19 December 1945.

"War Crimes Judges Heckle U.S. Effort to Convict 'Small Fry' Nazis as Group," San Francisco Examiner, 19 December 1945.

"Patton's Condition Slowly Improving," San Francisco Examiner, 19 December 1945.

"Denies He Confessed to Killing Girl, Tossing Corpse Off a Cliff," Daily News, published 30 December 1945.

"McMonigle's Wife Sues Him For Divorce," Hanford Sentinel, published 1 February 1946.

"M'Monigle Shaken As Wife's Divorce Papers Are Served," Oakland Tribune, 1 February 1946.

"This is Your Town by Jack Burroughs," Oakland Tribune, 1 February 1946.

"San Jose Woman May Have Seen Girl Kidnapped," Sacramento Bee, published 2 February 1946.

"Girl's Parents to Be First Witnesses in McMonigle Hearing," Santa Cruz Sentinel-News, published 3 February 1946.

"Thora Parent's Take Stand," Santa Maria Times, published 5 February 1946.

"McMonigle Trial Opens With Father's Testimony," Santa Maria Times, published 5 February 1946.

"Five of Girl's Schoolmates Identify Accused Slayer," Santa Cruz Sentinel-News, published 6 February 1946.

"M'Monigle Put On Witness Stand," Santa Cruz Sentinel-News, published 8 February 1946.

"Women In Rush To Get Seats in Courtroom," Santa Cruz Sentinel-News, published 8 February 1946.

"Newspaper Talent Here In Strength," Santa Cruz Sentinel-News, published 10 February 1946.

"Slayer Suspect Changes Story," Ventura County Star-Free Press, published 12 February 1946.

"McMonigle's Fifth Story Discounted," The Californian, published 12 February 1946.

"FBI Men Testifying in McMonigle Trial," Tulane Advance-Register, published 13 February 1946.

"Murder Jury to Witness Body Search," The Press Democrat, published 18 February 1946.

"McMonigle Found Guilty of Murder," Ventura County Star-FreePress, published 20 February 1946.

"Alton Man, Convicted in Murder, Shadowed Across U.S. for Weeks, FBI Files Show," St. Louis Star-Times, published 2 March 1946.

"Monterey Fisherman Is Still 'Dreaming' About Greer Garson's Rescue," The Californian, published 20 April 1946.

"Body of Second McMonigle Victim Found on Beach," The Californian, published 20 April 1946.

"McMonigle Trial To Reopen," Daily Review, published 20 April 1946.

"Mrs. Hogmire Disappears in Coastal Search," San Mateo Times, published 25 April 1946.

"News Behind the News," McClure News Syndicate published by San Mateo Times, 26 April 1946.

"Hogmire Thinks Wife May Be Kidnap Victim," San Mateo Times, published 26 April 1946.

"Search Fails Third Day For Mrs. Hogmire," San Mateo Times, published 27 April 1946.

"Woman's Body Found at Foot Of Coast Cliff," San Mateo Times, published 2 May 1946.

"Gang Murder in Hollywood," San Mateo Times, published 2 May 1946.

"Devil's Slide Victim's Mate Held For Quiz," San Francisco Examiner, published 3 May 1946.

"Wife of McMonigle Victim's Finder Added to List," San Francisco Examiner, published 3 May 1946.

"S.F. Junkman Still Quizzed In Wife's Death," San Mateo Times published 3 May 1946.

"Two Brothers Admit Attack on WAC Girls," San Mateo Times,

published 3 May 1946.

"Relatives of Dead Wife See Mate in Jail," San Mateo Times, published 6 May 1946.

"Lie Detector Backs Hogmire," San Mateo Times, published 8 May 1946.

"Lie Detector Test Backs Hogmire," San Francisco Examiner, published 9 May 1946.

"Hogmire Freed in Wife's Death," San Francisco Examiner, published 11 May 1946.

"Prison Warden Bans 'Resurrection' Attempt," Miami News, published 14 March 1947.

'Blind Girl Rejects McMonigle Offer of Eyes After Execution," Oakland Tribune, published 16 March 1947.

"Even a Sneeze May Start War, Rumors in Tokyo," Oakland Tribune, published 16 March 1947.

"Will Russia Declare War If U.S. Helps Greece? Asks Taft," Oakland Tribune, published 16 March 1947.

"France Urges Big 4 Reduce Reich Population for Peace," Oakland Tribune, published 16 March 1947.

"Hearing Today for M'Monigle," San Francisco Examiner, published 26 May 1947.

"McMonigle Eye Defects Denied," San Francisco Examiner, published 28 May 1947.

"New Murder Charge To Face M'Monigle," San Mateo Times, published 18 June 1947.

"Probationer Here, One of 12 in Gang Arrest," San Mateo Times, published 18 June 1947.

"McMonigle Wins 90-Day Stay," Santa Cruz Sentinel, published

19 June, 1947.

"McMonigle Loses Supreme Court Plea," Santa Cruz Sentinel, published 30 December 1947.

"More 'Maps' By McMonigle Cause Flurry," San Mateo Times, published 20 February 1948.

"M'Monigle Executed," San Mateo Times, published 20 February 1948.

"72 Witness McMonigle Death in Gas Chamber," San Francisco Examiner, published 21 February 1948.

"McMonigle Dies in Gas Chamber Denying Guilt, "San Francisco Examiner, published 21 February 1948.

"Triumphed," Daily News, published 18 April 1948.

Carl Nolte, "Bay Area mob lynched kidnappers 75 years ago," San Francisco Chronicle, published 23 November 2008.

"Cory's Historical Corner," The Sierra Prospect, posted 22 August 2018.

Other Sources:

California During World War II, Wikipedia
California After the War, Called To Action, California State Museum
Operation Magic Carpet, Wikipedia
Robert E. Cornish, Wikipedia
Japan-Russia Border, Wikipedia
Thora Afton Chamberlain, Charley Project
Federal Bureau of Investigation Law Enforcement Bulletin, September 1954.
FBI History Timeline
FBI Mission & Priorities, Frequently Asked Question
Missing Persons Commentary. blogspot.com
"Proclamation 2673: Thanksgiving Day 1945, The American

Presidency Project

San Francisco Bay Area Western Bands 1944-52, Country Music Archive.

Manor Theater newspaper ad published in The Times, 6 May 1946.

Britannica.com, definition of habeas corpus

ABOUT THE AUTHOR

Rod Kackley

It's all about the story, as far as Rod is concerned.

Whether it's Shocking True Crime Stories or one of his many works of fiction. Rod wants to keep you turning pages and reading incredible tales of criminals, their victims, and their capture.

Spoiler alert: No matter how long it takes, the bad guys rarely win. But it's the criminal who is often the most compelling character.

That's true whether it's "Mommy Deadliest," the story of a woman who kills her children, or "The Day Eva Dugan Died, the story of the last person hung for murder in Arizona.

In Rod's world of fiction, he spins yarns about "The Coffee Shoppe Killer, a woman who kills her lovers when they disappoint her.

A teenage girl wraps a serial killer around her finger in "Go Big or Go Dead."

Then there's "The Murder of Emma Brown," where two young women go out to party one night, and one only returns home.

Written in Kalamazoo, Michigan, Rod's books and stories allow his readers to brush up against the world of crime without getting hurt. And it's a heck of a ride!

For more go to rodkackley.com.

BOOKS BY THIS AUTHOR

The Day Eva Dugan Died: A Shocking True Crime Story

The Iowa Murders: A Shocking True Crime Story

88 Days: The Abduction Of Jayme Closs

#Justice For Ashley: A Shocking True Crime Story

Murder's Always Murder: Shocking True Crime Stories

Sealed With A Kill: A Shocking True Crime Love Story

Kalamazoo's Suitcase Killer: A Shocking True Crime Story

Never Forgive Never Forget: A Shocking True

Crime Story

She Deserved Better: A Shocking True Crime Story Of A Craigslist Killer

Never Again: An Internet Killer Thriller

Murder Is Best Served Bloody

The Murder Of Emma Brown

The Coffee Shoppe Killer: Inspired By A Shocking True Crime Story

Go Big Or Go Dead: A Serial Killer Thriller

Empty Minute: A Murder Mystery

Mommy Deadliest: A Shocking True Crime Story Of A Murdering Mother

Made in United States
North Haven, CT
11 March 2024